ACTS OF WORSHIP

W. B. J. MARTIN

ACTS OF WORSHIP

ABINGDON PRESS

new york
nashville

ACTS OF WORSHIP

Copyright © 1960 by Abingdon Press

Library of Congress Catalog Card Number: 60-10912

SET UP, PRINTED, AND BOUND BY THE
PARTHENON PRESS, AT NASHVILLE,
TENNESSEE, UNITED STATES OF AMERICA

TO MY WIFE

INTRODUCTION

I BELIEVE THAT ELEVEN O'CLOCK ON SUNDAY MORNING IS, or could be, the most important hour of the week. In this spirit I offer this little collection of worship material, in mingled gratitude and exasperation, to the Church that has provided me with some of the most exciting, and some of the dullest, hours of my life. I cannot agree with Professor Whitehead's famous remark, "Religion is what the individual does with his own solitariness," for when I am solitary, I am only half a person. What enriches me and encourages me to persist in the adventure of being a human being is the presence of the people of God. In this I am with John Wesley, who said, "The Bible knows nothing of solitary religion," and I gladly testify that I owe whatever spiritual vitality I possess to regular participation in the prayers and faith of the church. And yet I must confess that I have often been solitary in church, cut off from both preacher and the rest of the congregation. When I analyze this, I see that it is partly my own fault, but also it has been due partly to the absence of liturgical material that would draw me into the community of worship and plant me firmly in the midst of the gathered company. Believing that criticism should be positive, I offer this collection of prayers, creeds, and litanies as a small contribution to my fellow worshipers. I am bold enough to think that it possesses some distinctive features which, if adopted, would give people a greater sense of participation in the astonishing act we call "the service" of prayer and praise.

1. In the first section "Calls to Worship," I have gone to some length to avoid the merely religious and to concentrate on the Christian. I have sought for such sentences as will confront the worshiper with the offer of the gospel of Jesus Christ. When the opening Call to Worship is taken, as it often is, from the Old Testament, the full evangelical note of forgiveness and reconciliation is often muted, although, of course, there are Old Testament passages so haunting in their wooing note and so laden with evangelical associations that they cannot fail to awaken Christian worship. Again, I have sought for passages that spell out, as far as this is possible within the range of three or four sentences, what worship is and what it entails on the part of the

8

worshiper in terms of expectation and interior attitude. Some of these passages are biblical, some have
been supplemented with material taken from theo-
logians and saints, and some are writings that express
the essentially biblical message but do so in the idiom
of our own time, thus alerting the worshiper who has
become accustomed to over-familiar words.

In this section the "Calls to Worship" are followed
immediately by an invocatory prayer, which arises di-
rectly out of reflection on the preceding words. I per-
sonally like this arrangement, but in gatherings where
"Call" and "Invocation" are separated by a hymn, the
two parts can easily be detached.

2. Another distinctive feature is the inclusion of
several affirmations of faith and creedal statements,
and in particular, of *responsive* declarations of faith.
I have come to feel, after a long time in the ministry,
that the greatest lack in a service of worship is the
opportunity given to the gathered congregation to declare its faith. Nothing will rescue a congregation
from being a collection of specators like the stand-
ing on its feet to articulate its convictions before
God. One of the weaknesses, so it seems to the writer,
about the use of creedal statements, however, is that
the congregation is invited to declare only its *intellectual* convictions; that is why he has offered here
a responsive statement which attempts to be a *response,*
a declaration by the gathered company of its duties,

sins, aspirations, and attitudes, seen in the light of the faith newly called to its attention.

3. In the third section of the book I have written a series of meditations on biblical themes. The advantages of using a meditative form of congregational prayer have impressed themselves upon me with increasing force of late for two reasons:

a) The meditation invites people to base their prayers, thanksgiving, confession, intercession, and petition upon the Scriptures. A great saint was once asked about the respective merits of Bible reading and prayer. He is alleged to have answered that if he were shut up to a choice, he would unhesitatingly choose Bible reading, for, said he, the Bible always stirs up the desire to pray, whereas prayer by itself might lead the individual away from the distinctive claims and offers of the Bible.

b) Prayer that is based on the Bible will have the advantage of delivering men from their moods and subjectivisms; it will suggest to men many subjects, many needs and duties, many people and occasions for which they ought to pray; it will deepen their sense of sin and stir up within them unwonted aspirations. P. T. Forsyth put this in his usual arresting fashion when he said, "It is better and safer to pray over the Bible than to brood over self."

4. The same concentration on Scripture informs the next section of the book. I have tried to compose pas-

toral prayers that take their starting point not from the preacher's observations on the state of the world or his momentary sympathies but from the mission and message of Jesus Christ, and from what I call the imperatives of Jesus (i.e. the commissions which he entrusted, and still entrusts, to his followers).

5. In the fifth part I have been encouraged to include a series of litanies, a form of prayer which many find helpful, since it both provides matter for reflection and helps to create a sense of unity between the leader and the congregation. These are specially written with a view to reproduction in weekly bulletins or service papers.

6. The last section of the book is a collection of offertory prayers, written and used in the course of four pastorates. They attempt to bring the offering into the roughest, most realistic juxtaposition with the secular life of the worshiper, as well as to enlarge thought concerning the scope and extent of the church to which he belongs.

The appreciation accorded to this material in the actual life of the worshiping congregation encourages the author to share it with his brother ministers and with those responsible for leading prayer sessions in groups.

W. B. J. MARTIN

CONTENTS

SECTION IV
Pastoral Prayers Based on the Words of Jesus   129

CONTENTS

SECTION I

Calls to Worship
and
Prayers of Invocation

This is the message which we have heard of him, and declare unto you, that God is light, and in him is no darkness at all.

God is love and every one that loveth is born of God, and knoweth God.

God is a Spirit: and they that worship him must worship him in spirit and in truth.

God was in Christ, reconciling the world unto himself.

Let us pray:

O Lord our God, in this act of worship we glory in the light and love that have been made known to us in Jesus Christ. Come, O light divine, and dispel our human darkness! Come, O love divine, and win thy victory over our hard and loveless hearts! Make us children of the day and sons of the light, make us partners in thy strong, creative will for mankind. Reconcile us to ourselves, to our fellow men, and to thyself, who art our life.

Through Jesus Christ. AMEN.

This is the day which the Lord hath made; we will rejoice and be glad in it.

Thou shalt call the sabbath a delight . . . not doing thine own ways, nor finding thine own pleasure, nor speaking thine own words: but shalt thou delight thyself in the Lord.

Let us pray:

Thanks be unto thee, O God, for this day of rest and gladness, for the clean air of Sunday, for the "walk together to the kirk in a goodly company," for the Book to read from, for good words that liberate and quicken the mind, for leisure to enjoy the family and to replenish the soul.

Encourage us to use this day aright, to build up our spent stores of love and faith, to disinfect ourselves of evil, to repair our friendship with Jesus Christ. And grant that as it comes to its close, we may be able to say, "It was good for us that we went into the House of the Lord."

We ask this for Christ's sake. AMEN.

I was glad when they said unto me, Let us go into the house of the Lord.

Happy is he that hath the God of Jacob for his help, whose hope is in the Lord his God:

He will fulfil the desire of them that fear him: he also will hear their cry, and will save them.

Let us pray:

Holy Father, we enter into thy courts with thanksgiving and into thy gates with praise. Praise be to thee for the gift of Jesus Christ, from whom all blessing and thanksgiving flows. Praise be to thee for the light he sheds upon our human path, for the power he gives us to overcome and master temptation, and to live in fellowship with thee. Give us grace to share anew his victory over sin and death, to accept the forgiveness he offers, and to walk in his way.

And this we ask for his name's sake. AMEN.

I beseech you therefore, brethren, by the mercies of God, that ye present your bodies a living sacrifice, holy, acceptable unto God, which is your reasonable service.

. . . ye are not your own, for ye are bought with a price: therefore glorify God in your body, and in your spirit, which are God's.

Let us pray:

Almighty Father, most gladly we confess today that we are not our own. Many hands have gone to the fashioning of our lives, much love and tenderness have been poured upon us to bring us where we are today. And not human love only, but thy divine care and guardianship of us. We are what we are because thou art mindful of us, because thou didst create us and re-create us in Jesus Christ. Lord, it is impossible for us to live only for ourselves. Thou art calling us to be stewards of thy bounty, saying to each of us, "freely thou has received, freely give." AMEN.

Behold, I bring you good tidings of great joy.

For unto you is born . . . a Saviour, which is Christ the Lord.

Unto you it is given to know the mystery of the kingdom of God.

Unto you is given power above all that ye can ask or think.

Let us pray:

Almighty God, help us to rejoice today in the fulness and splendor of the gifts that are offered to us in thy gospel. Help us to worship in plenitude, to stretch forth our hands to receive, to welcome thy Son Jesus Christ into our cramped and restricted lives. Strike at the root of penury in our hearts, deliver us from living in poverty in the midst of plenty, and make us generous both in our receiving and our out-giving.

For Jesus' sake. AMEN.

When you come to worship the Lord exalt Him as much as you can.

Lift up your hearts.

Present your bodies a living sacrifice, . . . which is your reasonable service.

Let this mind be in you, which was also in Christ Jesus.

Let us pray:

Almighty God, we would offer and present ourselves unto thee this day: body, mind, and spirit. Let thy Holy Spirit so possess us that our bodies may glow with inward light, that our minds may respond to the truth with eager delight, that our hearts may overflow with forgiving love to all men. May the Incarnate Word suffuse our lives with his glory and may our obedience to his spoken words give weight and stability to all we do.

We ask this for his name's sake. AMEN.

Let thy delight be in the Almighty and lift up thy face unto God.

The Lord make his face shine upon thee, and be gracious unto thee.

(And) we all, . . . beholding as in a glass the glory of the Lord, are changed into the same image from glory to glory.

Let us pray:

Almighty and most merciful God, we lift our faces toward thee, for we live only as we receive thy blessing.

We thank thee that thy face is ever turned toward us, else we should know only the dark clouds of the wrath we have deserved. But praise be to thy generous love! Thou hast commanded the light to shine out of darkness and *into* the darkness, and we have seen thy glory in the face of Jesus Christ. Help us to stand where he can reach us, until we are transformed by the warmth of his love and the power of his forgiveness.

We ask it in his name. AMEN.

The good news of the kingdom of God.

Jesus said:
He hath anointed me to preach the gospel to the poor; . . .
to heal the broken-hearted,
to preach deliverance to the captives,
and recovering of sight to the blind,
to set at liberty them that are bruised,
to preach the acceptable year of the Lord.

Let us pray:
Almighty God, we gather in this house of prayer to open our lives to the good news, to learn to respond to the offer of health and joy and peace and sight and freedom. Forgive us if these things do not excite us— if we have become so accustomed to sickness, blindness, slavery that we regard them as normal—and show us, in thy Son Jesus Christ, what life might be, even for us, if we lived, as he did, in constant expectation of thy entry into our lives.

And this we ask for his name's sake. AMEN.

Behold, I bring you good tidings of great joy.

The Lord reigneth; let the earth rejoice.

The light shineth in darkness; and the darkness comprehended it not.

Where sin abounds, there grace much more abounds.

For God so loved the world, that he gave his only begotten Son, that whosoever believeth in him should not perish, but have everlasting life.

Let us pray:
Almighty God, we thank thee that we walk in the midst of so much assurance. Though our faith falter and our steps stumble, thy faithfulness abides and thy way is sure. As we gather today in thy sanctuary, help us to be aware of the grace wherein we stand, and deliver us from our human fears and from misplaced confidence in our own feelings. Grant that what thou hast done in Jesus Christ may become the source of our hope.

And this we ask for his name's sake. AMEN.

Rejoice in the Lord always: and again I say, Rejoice.

Be careful for nothing; but in every thing by prayer and supplication . . . let your requests be made known unto God.

And the peace of God, which passeth all understanding, shall keep your hearts and minds through Christ Jesus.

Let us pray:

Heavenly Father, we have carried with us into this house our cares, anxieties, and fears. Help us to lift them into thy presence and to see them against the spacious background of thy good purpose. Grant us a sense of proportion that we may see our temporary worries against thy permanent love and our selfish fears against thy everlasting righteousness.

And if we have come to worship without a care in the world, help us to offer thee our happiness and serenity, that it may be of service to thee. If we are enjoying vigorous health, joyful family relationships, the precious boon of a good conscience, and a quiet mind, help us to make these things a starting place for new endeavor and deeper commitment.

And this we ask for Jesus' sake. Amen.

Thy mercy, O Lord, is in the heavens; and thy faithfulness reacheth unto the clouds.

Thy righteousness is like the great mountains; thy judgments are a great deep.

How excellent is thy lovingkindness, O God! therefore the children of men put their trust under the shadow of thy wings.

Let us pray:

Almighty God, we stand amazed at the wonder of thy being. We are astonished at ourselves, that we make such poor and grudging response to thy love. Mercy, faithfulness, righteousness, lovingkindness— they are all ours for the asking! The infinite God waits upon our consent!

Lord, teach us to pray, to open our lives to thy generous gifts. Enlarge our hearts. Quicken our longing for a share of thy perfection. And this for no selfish end, but rather that we might have the wherewithal to share with others and to spend for the life of the world.

We ask these things for Jesus Christ's sake. Amen.

Jesus said:

Ask, and it shall be given you; seek, and ye shall find; knock, and it shall be opened unto you.

> "Thou art coming to a king;
> Large petitions with thee bring."

Expect great things from God, attempt great things for God.

Let us pray:

Lord, we rejoice that we are coming to One who is more concerned for our welfare than we are ourselves, more eager to give than we are to receive. We do not have to bully or cajole thee. It is our capacity to take that needs enlarging, our ambition to live off thy bounty that needs quickening. So we pray that today's encounter with Jesus Christ may rebuke our piecemeal, hand-to-mouth, shoddy living and set us hungering for the life that is life indeed.

And this we ask in his name. AMEN.

God is not far from every one of us, for in him we live and move, and have our being.

> "Closer is He than breathing,
> Nearer than hands or feet."

Jesus said: The Kingdom of God is at hand: repent ye, and believe the gospel.

Let us pray:

Heavenly Father, forgive us for seeking to dramatize ourselves as strugglers and searchers when all the time the kingdom is at our door. Forgive us for creating difficulties where none exist that we might postpone the act of decision. Forgive us for our blindness to thy obvious presence in our midst. Above all, forgive us for wanting a private sign when thy great public sign, thy Son Jesus Christ, waits upon our discovery.

Make us humble enough to repent, to turn about and change our attitude. Make us true believers— willing to attend to the good news and to act upon it.

We ask this for Christ's sake. AMEN.

When thou saidst, seek ye my face; my heart said unto thee, Thy face, Lord, will I seek.

The Lord make his face to shine upon thee, and be gracious unto thee.

We have seen the glory of God in the face of Jesus Christ. And we all, . . . beholding as in a glass the glory of the Lord, are changed into the same image from glory to glory.

Let us pray:

Almighty God, we praise thee that thou hast un-covered thy face in Jesus Christ, that in the human countenance of the Son we have seen the Father. We ourselves had no face until we reflected the face of our parents, our loved ones, and our friends; it is through them that we became human. Make us even more deeply human, rightly and richly human, by confronting us anew in Jesus Christ. May his compassionate eyes look upon us to our salvation.

> His kind but searching glance can scan
> The very wounds that shame would hide,

but in that glance alone is healing for our shame and peace for our restlessness. AMEN.

Behold, what manner of love the Father hath bestowed upon us, that we should be called the sons of God.

Herein is love, not that we loved God, but that he loved us, and sent his Son to be the propitiation for our sins.

While we were yet a great way off, the Father ran, and had compassion upon us.

We would not be seeking him had he not already found us.

Let us pray:

As we enter upon the hospitality of this house of prayer, we thank thee for the love that awaits us. We thank thee for thy faith in us, awakening faith; for thy hope creating hope in our despair; for thy presence that has never left us and now summons us to conscious and grateful fellowship with thyself. Before we called, thou didst answer, and while we were yet seeking, thou didst find us.

So we embark upon this act of worship, knowing that thou who didst begin a good work in us will complete it, and that thy patience will outwear our defections and wanderings. Lord, increase our faith!

Through Jesus Christ our Lord. AMEN.

Blessed is he whose transgression is forgiven, whose sin is covered.

As long as I refused to own my guilt, life ebbed away. My body dried up as in summer heat.

I acknowledged my sin unto thee, . . . I said, I will confess my transgressions unto the Lord; and thou forgavest the iniquity of my sin.

Let us pray:

Almighty and most merciful God, we thank thee for this opportunity of confession and renewal. We have carried about with us the burden of memory and regret, of failure and remorse, and it has sapped our vitality and made us languid in service and feeble in witness.

Help us now to acknowledge our transgressions and to face with utter honesty the evasions, compromises, and cowardices of which we have been guilty. We believe it is thy will for us to rise on stepping-stones of our dead selves to better things, to learn from the mistakes of the past, and to live in firm dependence upon thee. To this end we open our lives anew to the coming of thy searching light.

Through Jesus Christ our Lord. Amen.

All things are of God, who hath reconciled us to himself by Jesus Christ.

For all things are yours; Whether . . . the world, or life, or death, or things present, or things to come; all are yours; And ye are Christ's; and Christ is God's.

It is the Father's good pleasure to give you the kingdom.

Let us pray:

Heavenly Father, help us to take our rightful place in the world today not as slaves fearful of a master, nor as servants giving grudging obedience, but as sons and daughters rejoicing in a father's love.

We believe that thou hast destined us for plenitude not poverty, for victory not defeat, for mastery over events and circumstances not capitulation to them; help us, then, to share in the victory of Christ. Help us to take him at his word and to make this service an hour of decision, the decision to live in fellowship with him and to enter with him into possession of thy grace and strength.

And this we ask in his name. AMEN.

Grace be to you, and peace, from God our Father, and from the Lord Jesus Christ.

Blessed be the God and Father of our Lord Jesus Christ, who hath blessed us with all spiritual blessings . . . in whom we have redemption through his blood, the forgiveness of sins, according to the riches of his grace.

Let us pray:

Most merciful Father, we thank thee for thy lavish generosity to us, the children of men. We who deserve nothing but judgment are called this day into fellowship with thee through thy Son Jesus Christ. We stand in perpetual amazement of thy love, manifested in the life and death and resurrection of Jesus Christ, else we could not believe it. But thou hast placarded it before our eyes. Thanks be to thee! Help us now to abandon our craven fears and to turn in faith to the love revealed on Calvary. Suffer us not to rely upon our own feelings, but give us courage to trust what we have seen in his outstretched arms, the love that will not let us go.

And this we ask for his sake. AMEN.

The Spirit and the bride say, Come. And let him that heareth say, Come. And let him that is athirst come. And whosoever will, let him take of the water of life freely. . . . Even so, come, Lord Jesus.

Let us pray:

Almighty God, we pray that this service of worship may be an event in our lives, not simply the rehearsal of a familiar habit but an encounter with our living Lord. May our prayers rise to thee out of our deep need, not from our surface wants. Provoke in us a thirst for the water of life that we may cry welcome to thee with outstretched hands, as men and women who know that their lives are parched and dry without thee. And where we cannot, through the weakness of sin, reach out to grasp thee, do thou grasp us by thy strong hand and lead us to the fountains of living waters.

And this we ask for Jesus Christ's sake. AMEN.

Is any among you afflicted? let him pray.

Is any merry? let him sing psalms.

If any have committed sins, they shall be forgiven him.

Confess your faults one to another, and pray for one another, that ye may be healed.

Let us pray:
O God, who hast wonderfully enriched our human lives by calling us into the fellowship of thy Son's Church and hast strengthened us by the prayers and encouragement of our fellow Christians, help us now to pray for one another. May this service today lift the burden from the afflicted, giving them confidence in the healing power of Christ; may it purify and deepen the merriment of the glad, enlisting it for the building up of the people of God, and may it assist the conscience-stricken and the penitent to acknowledge and renounce their sins.

Since there is none righteous—no, not one—grant us courage to confess our common guilt and thereby to seek a common salvation in Christ Jesus.

We ask it in his name. AMEN.

O come, let us worship and bow down.

Worship is thinking magnificently about God.[1]

Worship is the willingness to be commanded by God.[2]

Worship is man's response to God's gift in Jesus Christ.

Let us pray:

Almighty God, our Heavenly Father, make this act of worship an event in our lives. May it be an experience that cleanses us at the very center of our being, freshening the springs of life, probing the hidden depths of many a heart, searching our secret sins, and purifying our aims and ambitions.

As we stay here, singing, praying, and listening, let thy great hand shape our lives, let Christ thy Son claim us anew for himself, and let the Holy Spirit revive and empower us.

And this we ask for Jesus Christ's sake. AMEN.

[1] A. J. Gossip, "In the Secret Place of the Most High."
[2] James Reid, "The Victory of God."

O come, let us worship and bow down.

In worship we behold the Goodness of God and become partakers of that goodness.

In worship we see the patience of God and become possessed by that patience.

In worship we glimpse the Purpose of God and enlist in that purpose.

In worship we meet the Power of God and stand in its strengthening.[3]

Let us pray:
Lord our God, we bow in adoration before thy greatness. Enable us to let go of our littleness, our small achievements, and our timid purposes that we may be taken up into thy ambitious purpose for us. We believe it is thy will that all thy children should live in fullness of joy and love and peace. Lord, we believe; help thou our unbelief!

And this we ask in the name of Jesus Christ. AMEN.

[3] Adapted from the writings of Nels Ferré.

Let us worship God.

Worship is the nourishment of the mind upon God's truth.

It is the quickening of the conscience by His holiness.

It is the cleansing of the imagination by His beauty.

It is the enlargement of the heart through His love.[4]

Let us pray:

Lord our God, we could place our lives where they might become available to thee, open to all the movements of thy Spirit and the generosity of thy gifts.

Take our minds that they may think thy thoughts after thee; alarm and arouse our sleeping consciences; make us sensitive to the beauty of holiness and the holiness of beauty, and flood our narrow hearts with thy great love in Jesus Christ.

And this we ask for his name's sake. AMEN.

[4] Adapted from William Temple.

Into thy hands we commend our spirits.

It is a fearful thing to fall into the hands of the living God.
But it is a much more fearful thing to fall out of them.

.   .   .   .

Save me, O God, from falling into the ungodly knowledge
of myself as I am without God.
Let me never know, O God
let me never know what I am or should be
when I have fallen out of your hands, the hands of the
   living God.[5]

Let us pray:

We thank thee, O Father, for thy strong and sure
hands grasping our lives, soothing us in sorrow, smit-
ing us in rebellion, guiding us in uncertainty, shading
us in the noonday glare. Sometimes we rebel against
thy pressure upon our lives and shrug thee off and
run into darkness and danger. But ever and anon we
are brought back, for thou hast the Good Shepherd's
hands; ever and anon we are picked up and mended,
for thou hast the Carpenter's hands; ever and anon
we are drawn back home, for thou hast the hands
of our Father. Thanks be to thee, O God. AMEN.

[5] D. H. Lawrence, *Collected Poems*, III, 142.

Cast thy burden upon the Lord, and he shall sustain thee.

"Religion is no more a burden to man than wings are to a bird, than sails are to a ship." [6] Prayer is the spread of life to catch the winds of God. "In Him we live and move and have our being."

Let us pray:

Almighty God, may this hour of worship be an adventure of the spirit wherein we throw aside our fears and launch our craft upon thy safe seas. We believe that in thy service there is perfect freedom, that in thy presence there is fulness of joy. Help us, then, to live upon thy abundant resources, offered so freely to mankind in Jesus Christ thy Son.

We ask this in his name. AMEN.

[6] Samuel Rutherford, *Letters.*

Lift up your hearts.

We lift them up unto the Lord. . . .

It is very meet, right, and our bounden duty, that we should at all times and in all places, give thanks unto thee, O Lord, Holy Father, Almighty, Everlasting God.

Therefore with Angels and Archangels, and with all the company of heaven, we laud and magnify thy glorious Name; evermore praising thee, and saying, HOLY, HOLY, HOLY, Lord God of hosts.[7]

Let us pray:
Lord, we set our prayers today within the context of thy great Church, the Church militant here on earth and the Church triumphant in heaven. With all thy saints, living and departed, obscure and famous, we lift up our hearts in gratitude for Jesus Christ, the great Head of the Church, by whose life and death and resurrection she is continually recreated and reformed. Make us better members of this fellowship to which we are pledged, and enable us to affirm continually, by word and deed and thought, our membership of the whole Church throughout the world. AMEN.

[7] The Book of Common Prayer, Communion Service, pp. 76-77.

O magnify the Lord with me, and let us exalt his name together.

In His will is our peace.[8]

In His service there is perfect freedom.[9]

In His presence there is fulness of joy.

In seeking Him we find ourselves.

Let us pray:

Almighty God, we seek in this act of worship to be found by thee, for without thee we are lost.

We seek in fellowship, for we are most truly ourselves when we are at-one with our fellow men.

We seek in confidence, since we know from Jesus thy Son that thou art already seeking us.

We seek in penitence, for we realize how often we have ignored thy presence and deliberately walked in darkness.

We seek in hope, the hope that thou wilt use our seeking and finding to enrich the world in which we live.

Through Jesus Christ our Lord. AMEN.

[8] Dante.
[9] Augustine.

Praise ye the Lord!

The glorious company of the apostles praise Him.
The goodly fellowship of the prophets praise Him.
The noble army of martyrs praise Him.
The holy church throughout all the world doth acknowledge Him.

Therefore with angels and archangels and all the company of heaven, we laud and magnify His holy Name.[10]

Let us pray:

Lord our God, all creation sings thy praise. Shall we, thy children, formed in thine image, withhold our voices? "Break, my soul, thy guilty silence!"

Release in us now the spirit of praise, and may praise sweep through our lives, cleansing and invigorating them and opening them to the further incoming of thy love.

This we ask for Jesus Christ's sake. AMEN.

[10] "Te Deum."

What is the chief end of man?

The chief end of man is to glorify God and to enjoy Him for ever.[11]

Man was created to love, reverence, and serve God.[12]

Turn back, O man, forswear thy foolish ways.[13]

Let us pray:

Almighty God, our Maker and Owner, we bow in prayer to remember why we were created, to whom we belong, for what purpose thy love fashioned us and continually sustains us. We believe that we are truly human, truly fulfilling our destiny, only when we love, reverence, and serve thee, when all our deeds and all our days sing to thy glory. Forgive us our aimless living; forgive us for all the hours we have wasted in indecision, in serving the momentary impulses of our own hearts. Like the prodigal father, run forth to meet us now in this act of worship and reinstate us in the family to which we rightly belong.

We ask this for Christ's sake. AMEN.

[11] The Shorter Catechism.
[12] *Spiritual Exercises of St. Ignatius.*
[13] Clifford Bax.

God created man in his own image—and our hearts are restless till they find rest in him.

God created man in righteousness—and in his will is our peace.

God created man for obedience—and in his service there is perfect freedom.

Let us pray:

Almighty God, our Creator, who knowest us better than we know ourselves, and whose will for us far surpasses in splendor and joy anything that we devise or imagine for ourselves, inspire us to surrender our restlessness to thy peace, our futile self-will to thy creative purpose, and our foolish independence to thy sustaining and directing love. In this hour of worship lift us out of our petty concerns and give new depth and dignity to our lives by enlisting us again for thy kingdom, permitting us to share both the trials and triumphs, both the responsibilities and empowerments that come from fellowship with thy Son Jesus Christ.

And this we ask in his name. AMEN.

We bind unto ourselves today the strong name of the Trinity.[14]

We believe in one God the Father Almighty, Maker of heaven and earth. . . . and in one Lord Jesus Christ, the only-begotten Son of God; . . . we believe in the Holy Ghost, The Lord, and Giver of Life.

Let us pray:

Almighty God, help us to make this service an affirmation of faith and trust. Thou art our Father, and we belong to thee; only in thy presence are we genuinely human. Thou art our Maker and Owner; only in response to thy creative love are we capable of creation. We believe that Jesus Christ is mighty to save, and that we stand in constant need of his redeeming grace. We believe in thy Spirit, quickening life in all things, vivifying the stale stuff of tradition and habit, and leading us into new conquests. Yet we are here today, not because we believe in thee, but because thou dost believe in us; help us to stand in that faith.

For Jesus Christ's sake. AMEN.

[14] St. Patrick's Breastplate.

Enter into his gates with thanksgiving, and into his courts with praise.

> Let no unworthy thought
> Enter thy musing mind;
> Things which the world hath wrought,
> Untrue, unclean, unkind,
> Leave these behind.[15]

Let us pray:

Lord God, help us this day to put aside all miserable, grudging, and uncharitable thoughts. Help us to wash our minds clean with great acts of praise, to liberate ourselves from the bondage of self-pity by remembering what thou hast done for us in Jesus Christ. If we have carried into this house of prayer resentment, bitter memories, thoughts of revenge, malicious intentions, then, Lord, in thy mercy, sweeten our bitter-thoughted hearts with charity like thine. AMEN.

[15] Toc H prayer.

Jesus said, Wonder at the things before you, for he that wonders shall reign.[16]

> Give me miraculous eyes to see my eyes,
> Those rolling mirrors made alive in me,
> Terrible crystals more incredible
> Than all the things they see.[17]

Let us pray:

Almighty God, keep us in perpetual amazement of the miracle of our daily life that we may stand astonished at thy goodness, that we may be saved from taking thy care and love for granted. When we grow blasé, Lord, "Thy most pointed pleasure take, and stab our spirits broad awake."

Especially, we pray for a constant sense of wonder at the gift of thy Son Jesus Christ. "O the depth of the riches, both of the wisdom and knowledge of God! How unsearchable are His judgements, and His ways past finding out." Thanks be to thee, O God. AMEN.

---

[16] *Lost Sayings of Christ.*
[17] G. K. Chesterton, "The Sword of Surprise." Reprinted by permission of Dodd, Mead & Company from *The Collected Poems of G. K. Chesterton.* Copyright, 1932 by Dodd, Mead & Company. Used by permission of Miss D. E. Collins and Methuen & Co.

Prepare to meet thy God.

> Since we are coming to that holy room
> Where, with thy choir of saints for evermore
> We shall be made one music,
> We tune the instrument here by the door,
> And what we would do there
> Do here before.[18]

Let us pray:

Almighty God, we seek in this moment of worship to be made accessible to thee. We are common clay until thou dost breathe upon us; we are harsh and discordant until thy hand plucks music from our lives. So we bring our disordered lives, our rambling thoughts, our contradictory desires, our divided hearts and pray that thou wilt create stillness within us. Then in thy goodness give thyself to us, without whom nothing within us is holy, nothing is strong, nothing is pure. AMEN.

[18] John Donne, "Hymne to God My God, in My Sicknesse."

Forsake not the assembling of yourselves together.

When I came into the silent assemblies of God's people, I felt a secret power among them which touched my heart; and, as I gave way to it, I found the evil weakening in me, and the good raised up.[19]

Let us pray:

Lord Jesus Christ, who hast promised that where two or three are gathered together in thy name thou wilt be there in the midst, turn this gathering into an assembly of power. Break down the last lingering thoughts of evil within our hearts, raise up and nourish and strengthen the good that is struggling to be born within us. Help us to enrich this gathering of worshiping folk by bringing to it the deepest affirmation of our belonging.

And this we ask in thy Son's name. AMEN.

[19] Robert Barclay, Witness 343.

Whatsoever things are pure, whatsoever things are lovely, whatsoever things are of good report . . . think on these things . . . and the God of peace shall be with you.

For all emotions that are tense and strong,
    And utmost knowledge, let us live for these—
Live deep, and let the lesser things live long.[20]

Let us pray:
    Almighty God, who hast bidden us love thee with all our mind, fill our minds this day with enriching and liberating thoughts. Help us to cast aside whatsoever is impure, whatsoever is unlovely, whatsoever is of bad report—all that is merely critical, negative, destructive, and depressing. We pray that the mind which was also in Christ Jesus may also be in us—a mind uplifted towards thee, cleansed from self-seeking, suffused with grateful wonder.

We ask this for his name's sake. AMEN.

[20] Ernest Raymond, "Tell England" (New York: Doubleday & Company, Inc.). Used by permission of Ernest Raymond and Cassell.

Be still, and know that he is God.

> Think you 'mid this mighty sum
> Of things forever speaking
> That nothing of itself will come,
> But we must still be seeking? [21]

Let us pray:

Lord, we have come out of a world where things have shouted at us, bullied us into listening, competed for our attention, bribed us with the hope of glittering prizes. And now we find ourselves in the shy and delicate world of the spirit, where nothing shouts. Here nothing is revealed except to the humble and contrite. And we confess that we are not humble, though we would like to be—deeply and truly humble, humble enough to bow to the authority of truth and goodness and beauty. We confess that we are not contrite, though we are often sorry—sorry for ourselves and our miserable failures. Make us genuinely contrite, aware that the sins we commit are done against thee and thy purpose of love. Then, Lord, in thy mercy, enable us to respond to the meanings we shall find in the world about us, to open our lives to the healing and renewal that thou art offering us.

This we ask for Christ's sake. AMEN.

[21] Wordsworth.

The mercy of the Lord is from everlasting to ever-lasting. . . . Though we be faithless, He remaineth faithful, for He cannot be untrue to Himself.

> The One remains, the many change and pass;
> Heaven's light forever shines, Earth's shadows fly;
> Life, like a dome of many-colored glass,
> Stains the white radiance of Eternity.[22]

Let us pray:

Almighty and eternal God, we rejoice that our changing days are held in thy unchanging purpose. We bless thee that the white radiance of eternity trans-figures our common life, that ever and anon the dull-ness and dinginess of time is shot through with un-earthy gleams and that human love is suffused with a splendor that lifts us toward thee. For all intimations of immortality we give thee thanks; for every pull of the heart upwards, for every deep human experience that rends the veil of the commonplace, we bless thy name. But especially we praise thee for disclosing thy changeless and unsullied love in Jesus Christ thy Son. To him we turn now in this act of prayer; we open life to his transforming light. AMEN.

[22] Percy Bysshe Shelley, "Adonais."

Out of the depths have I cried unto thee, O Lord.
Lord, hear my voice.

> In the deserts of the heart
> Let the healing fountain start,
> In the prison of his days
> Teach the free man how to praise.[23]

Let us pray:

O God, our heavenly Father, we pray for a renewal of our inner life. We are tired of living on the
surface of things, and yet we lack the power to respond to thee from our deep inward center. Stir us up,
we beseech thee, that the poverty of our inner life
might become plenitude. So fill us with the abundance of thy grace that the wilderness of our lives
might become a spring of healing waters and that
the dirges of slavery might give place to the praises
of free men.

Deep calleth unto deep! May the deep of thy great
love speak to our emptiness and shallowness till we
rise empowered and blessed. AMEN.

[23] W. H. Auden, "In Memory of W. B. Yeats." Copyright
1940 by W. H. Auden. Reprinted from *The Collected Poetry of
W. H. Auden* by permission of Random House, Inc.

Jesus said: Lo, I am with you alway even unto the end of the world.

Raise the stone and thou shalt find me, cleave the wood and there I am.[24]

> The angels keep their ancient places;—
> Turn but a stone and start a wing!
> 'Tis ye, 'tis your estranged faces,
> That miss the many-splendored thing.[25]

Let us pray:

Almighty God, heaven and earth are full of thy glory; we walk knee-deep in miracle through the world that thou hast created. Forgive the blindness that misses the splendor all around us; forgive the eyes that search for thee on the far horizon and fail to observe thee close at hand; forgive the childishness that expects revelation in the unusual and spectacular and ignores the daily round, the common task as material for thy self-disclosure.

> Two worlds are ours,
> 'Tis only sin forbids us to descry
> The mystic heaven and earth within
> Plain as the sea and sky.[26]

AMEN.

[24] *Lost Sayings of Jesus.*
[25] Francis Thompson, "In No Strange Land."
[26] George Herbert.

Jesus said: Men ought always to pray, and not to faint.

O do not pray for easy lives, pray to be stronger men. Do not pray for tasks equal to your powers, but for powers equal to your tasks. Then the doing of your work shall be no miracle, but you will be the miracle. Every day you shall wonder at yourself and the richness of life which has come to you by the grace of God.[27]

Let us pray:

O Lord our God, strengthen us in this hour of worship to throw away the coward in our souls and to pray for heroic and adventurous living. Help us to say: "We expect great things from God; we will attempt great things for God," not because we boast of our own strength, but because we know the power of Christ to liberate and strengthen those who live in his presence.

And this we ask for his name's sake. AMEN.

[27] Phillips Brooks, *Visions and Tasks*, p. 330.

Seek ye the Lord while he may be found,
call ye upon him while he is near.

To all who are weary and seek rest,
To all who struggle and desire victory,
To all who sin and need a Saviour,
To all who are idle and look for service,
This hour is open with opportunity and promise.

Thou art coming to a King, large petitions with thee bring.[28]

Let us pray:
Lord, we thank thee for the hospitality of this house of prayer, for the wide-open arms of thy love welcoming us to seek newness of life. Thou alone knowest the need that has driven us into this place, and thou alone canst meet it. But there are needs of which we are, as yet, not conscious. May thy Son Jesus Christ illumine our lives today by his magnificent life, and in the light of that life may we become conscious of our hidden needs. Create in us a hunger and thirst after righteousness, after passionate purity, after whole-hearted dedication to thy will. AMEN.

[28] George Herbert, "The Church Porch."

Come, and let us return unto the Lord.

Return to the deep sources, nothing less
Will nourish the torn spirit, the bewildered heart,
The angry mind: and from the ultimate duress
Pierced with the breath of anguish, speak for love.

.   .   .   .

Return to the most human, nothing less
Will teach the angry spirit, the bewildered heart,
The torn mind to accept the whole of its duress
And, pierced with anguish, at last act for love.[29]

Let us pray:

Almighty God, we believe that the deepest things
within us are being stirred up in this act of worship,
that down below the surface of our lives thy spirit
strives with us to bring forth the men and women we
ought to be. Wrestle with us until we are overcome by
thy righteousness and conquered by thy love.

For Christ's sake. AMEN.

---

[29] "Santos; New Mexico." From *The Lion and the Rose* by
May Sarton. Copyright, 1948, by May Sarton. Reprinted by permission of Holt, Rinehart and Winston, Inc., *Atlantic Monthly*,
and the author.

When ye come to worship the Lord, exalt Him as much as ye can.

I say no man has ever yet been half devout enough;
None has ever yet adored or worship'd half enough;
. . . .

I say that the real and permanent grandeur of These
    States must be their Religion;
Otherwise there is no real and permanent grandeur;
Nor character, nor life worthy the name, without
    Religion;
Nor land, nor man or woman, without Religion.[30]

Let us pray:

    Almighty God, we summon up all that is within us to praise thy holy name. We would worship thee today not only with our lips but with our lives, not only with our minds but with our bodies, not only with our hearts but with our instincts, dreams, and desires. But these are brave words! Make them a living reality by fusing our disordered lives into one passionate unity, into one cry for help, one shout of praise.

    Through Jesus Christ our Lord. AMEN.

[30] Walt Whitman, "Starting from Paumanok."

There is a moment in the act of worship when neither the cry of penitence nor the hymn of adoration will satisfy—when the soul must launch forth in triumphant affirmation against all that is irrational, senseless and dark in the world. Then, to say "I believe" becomes the noblest act of which man is capable.

To such a moment we have come. [31]

Let us pray:

Heavenly Father. Why, the very words commit us to an act of faith! Here and now we commit ourselves, to take sides against all that is unheavenly, all that thwarts and denies thy holy will, all that mocks and caricatures thy fatherhood.

Enlist us, we beseech thee, for thine own gracious purposes for mankind. Equip us to fight against all that is base and ugly and mean. Show us where we may lay hold on the power to resist evil with good, to break down the hardness of men's hearts, and to transform foes into friends and friends into fellow workers in thy kingdom.

And this we ask for Jesus Christ's sake. AMEN.

[31] Adapted from L. P. Jacks, *The Alchemy of Thought* (London: Williams & Norgate, 1910), pp. 318-20. Used by permission of Ernest Benn Limited.

Choose you this day whom ye will serve.

There shall be always the Church and the World
And the Heart of Man
Shivering and fluttering between them, choosing and
chosen,
Valiant, ignoble, dark and full of light
Swinging between Hell Gate and Heaven Gate.
And the Gates of Hell shall not prevail.[32]

Let us pray:

Almighty God, we thy creatures need to be won again and again for thy Church and thy Kingdom. We have promised—and we have betrayed thee. We have offered thee our loyalty—and withdrawn it again. We are men and women in whom splendor and shame are strangely mixed. Yet we return ever and anon, for we cannot keep away from thee. Thou hast the words of eternal life. To whom then can we go but unto thee?

Accept this renewal of our worship this day, and keep us by thy strong grace.

We ask this for Jesus Christ's sake. AMEN.

[32] T. S. Eliot, "The Rock." Copyright 1934 by Harcourt, Brace and Co., Inc. Reprinted with their permission and that of Faber and Faber, Ltd.

The earth is the Lord's, and the fulness thereof.

Your enjoyment of the world is never right, till every morning you awake in heaven: see yourself in your Father's palace, and look upon the skies, the earth and the air as celestial joys.

You never enjoy the world aright till you perceive yourself to be the heir of the world; till you can rejoice and delight in God as misers do in gold, and kings in sceptres.[33]

Let us pray:

Almighty Father, help us to take possession of the world this day, not as slaves but as sons. We believe that thou hast given it to us for our use and delight, to enjoy it, to profit by it, to share it with others, and to find thee within it.

Forgive us if, through our sin and selfishness, we turn thy palace into a slum, if we make the wide world of freedom a prison, and grant that today we may turn from our sins to seek the forgiveness that can make us free men again.

And this we ask for Jesus' sake. AMEN.

[33] Thomas Traherne.

O come and let us return unto the Lord; for he hath torn, and he will heal us; he hath smitten and he will bind us up. Seek him that maketh the seven stars and Orion, that turneth the shadow of death into the morning . . . the Lord is his name.

Let us pray:

Almighty God, accept us now as we return to thee, who art the Lord of our lives. We have discovered thy lordship in frustration and disobedience, for whenever we have ignored thee our lives have gone awry. Help us now to discover thee in fulfillment and joy, as we gratefully acknowledge thy claim to our lives and seek to honor it with our obedience. Rescue us from the shadow of death, and from the crippling results of self-centered living, and fill us with the strength and health of thy presence. We ask this in Jesus' name. AMEN.

SECTION II

Affirmations of Faith

A Responsive Affirmation of Faith—I

Minister: As members of the Christian church let us affirm the things most surely believed among us, that we may apprehend with all the saints what is the length and breadth and height and depth of the love of God that passeth knowledge, and that we may open our lives anew to the riches of the everlasting gospel.

Minister: We believe in one God, the Father almighty, Maker of heaven and earth.

People: **Lord, we believe; help thou our unbelief. May the unity of God, righteous and loving, unify our broken lives.**
May the fatherhood of God establish us in true sonship.
May the creative love of God flow through our human works.

Minister: We believe in Jesus Christ, his only Son, our Lord.

People: **Lord, we believe; help thou our unbelief. In the life of Christ help us to seek our true humanity.**

In the Cross of Christ may we die to self and the world.
In the resurrection of Christ may we share his victory over sin and death.

Minister: We believe in the Holy Spirit, the Lord and Giver of life.

People: Lord, we believe; help thou our unbelief.
By the spirit of truth we would be led into all truth.
By the spirit of holiness we would be cleansed of all unrighteousness.
By the spirit of fellowship we would be redeemed from isolation.

Minister: We believe in the Holy Catholic Apostolic Church.

People: Lord, we believe; help thou our unbelief.
In the Holy Church may we recover our wholeness.
In the Catholic Church may we share our partial insights in love.
In the Apostolic Church make us witnesses and servants of all mankind.

Minister: We believe in the Kingdom of God, open to all who turn in trust and hope to receive it, where there is neither Jew nor Gentile, bond nor free, male nor female.

People: Lord, we believe; help thou our unbelief.

In the Kingdom of peace, make us all peace-makers.

In the Kingdom of love, endue us with power to forgive and restore.

In the Kingdom of joy create in us liveliness of mind and heart.

Minister: We believe in the life everlasting.

People: Lord, we believe; help thou our unbelief.

May life eternal fulfill and transform our passing days.

May the Resurrection hope give us victory over despair.

May the life everlasting bring us into unbroken fellowship with thee.

A Responsive Affirmation of Faith—II

Minister: We believe in one God, present in nature as law, in history as purpose, in society as fellowship, in man as creativity, and in Jesus Christ as redeeming love.

People: We believe that this is our Father's world,

the gift of his love, and that he wills that all men should come to the knowledge of himself.

Minister: We believe that the Bible testifies to the God who spoke, and still speaks, and who summons us to listen to his living word in the events of our own time.

People: **We believe that he has not left himself without witness and has given us the spirit of interpretation and obedience.**

Minister: We believe that human life is a dialogue with God and that he speaks in the call of duty, in the demand for integrity, in the claims of community, and in the struggle for growth and meaning.

People: **We believe that we are called to answer him in obedience, compassion, and creative struggle, and by responding to his gift in Christ.**

Minister: We believe in the Church, the people of God, created in Christ Jesus and called to embody his love and to express his purpose.

People: **We believe that we are called to the ministry of reconciliation and are empowered by his spirit to witness and evangelize.**

Minister: We believe in eternal life, already present

in every meaningful and loving act and offered to us in its fulness in Jesus Christ, both here and hereafter.

People: **We believe in the communion of saints and in the power of the resurrection to create all things new.**

All: **Amen.**

A Responsive Affirmation of Faith Based on the Lord's Prayer

Minister: We believe in God the Father of all, made known to us in the face of Jesus Christ, whose perfect Sonship invites us to live in filial trust and obedience.

People: **As God's children we renew our faith in his providence; we trust in his grace and seek to realize the brotherhood of man.**

Minister: We believe that God is our heavenly Father, our Creator, Judge, and Redeeming Lord. who wills our highest good.

People:　**As children of the highest we seek to culti-
vate the spirit of reverence and godly fear;
we repudiate the temptation to exploit
God for our own ends.**

Minister:　We believe that God's name is holy and that
all life is hallowed where his name is known
and revered.

People:　**As children of God we will seek to hallow
his name in reverent thought, in honest
speech, and in righteous deeds.**

Minister:　We believe that the kingdom of God is in
our midst, for Jesus Christ has opened the
kingdom of Heaven to all believers by his
obedient life, atoning death, and triumphant resurrection.

People:　**As heirs of the Kingdom, we repent and
believe the good news; we resolve to live
within its power, accepting its joy and de-
lighting in its laws.**

Minister:　We believe that God's will shall be done
on earth as it is done in heaven.

People:　**As citizens of the Kingdom we seek to make
the kingdoms of this world responsive and
obedient to Christ our Lord, that his will
may be done in business, commerce, culture,
and home.**

Minister: We believe that our daily bread is God's gift, and that our health and strength, our security and satisfaction are dependent upon his providence.

People: **As God's children we resolve to eat our bread with thanksgiving, to share it with others, and to resist the temptation to hoard our possessions.**

Minister: We believe in the forgiveness of sins and in the power of prayer to redeem the past and secure the future.

People: **As God's children we accept his pardon and cast our burden upon his forgiving grace lest we cripple life by fruitless remorse. We believe it is God's will for us to walk in fellowship with him.**

Minister: We believe that God's forgiveness enables us to show forgiveness to others, and that human forgiveness opens the way for his presence in our lives.

People: **As God's children we seek to share the understanding, compassion, and restoration that God has offered to us in his Son Jesus Christ.**

Minister: We believe that God does not suffer us to be tempted beyond our strength, that he is able to deliver them that are tempted.

74

People: **As children of God we accept the temptations that visit us as reminders of our absolute dependence upon him, and will turn to him for strength and renewal.**

Minister: We believe that it is God's will to deliver us from evil and to present us faultless before his glory in Jesus Christ our Lord.

People: **As God's children we recognize and repudiate the evil of hate, vindictiveness, inertia, greed, and fear and seek to overcome them by God's grace.**

All: **We believe that the Kingdom, the power, and the glory belong to God.**
O Lord, in thee we trust.
Let us never be confounded.

AMEN.

A Responsive Affirmation of Faith in Jesus Christ

Minister: We believe that Jesus of Nazareth is the Christ, the Son of the living God.

People: **We believe that in his human life of surrender to God's will and response to man's need we are shown the pattern for all human life. "In him was life, and the life was the light of men."**

Minister: We believe that he grew in favor with God and with man by discharging his responsibilities to nation, church, and family, within the will of God.

"Though he was a son, he learned obedience through the things he suffered."

People: **We believe that in his words of wisdom we hear the voice of God speaking to us, rebuking our half-truths, convicting us of error, and leading us into the fulness of truth.**

"Never spake man like this man."

Minister: We believe that in his works of healing his own compassion and the passion of God to restore what is maimed and broken were at one. "He healed all who had need of healing."

People: **We believe that in his compassion for sinners we see and experience the mercy of God and are shown how we ought to love the outcast and the lost. "He came to seek and to save that which was lost."**

Minister: We believe that at his baptism he was identified with all who struggled out of darkness toward the light. "He who knew no sin became sin for us."

People: **We believe that in his temptation in the wilderness we see the meaning and purpose of our temptations and are empowered to meet them. "He was tempted in all points like as we are, yet without sin."**

Minister: We believe that on his cross the mighty opposites of man's sin and God's grace clashed and were resolved. "Where sin abounds, there grace much more abounds." We believe that "he was wounded for our transgressions and bruised for our iniquities, and by his stripes we are healed."

People: **We believe that his resurrection is the victory over sin and death, and that "because he lives, we shall live also."**

Minister: We believe in his continuing presence with us in the world and the church. "Lo, I am with you alway, even unto the end of the age."

AMEN.

A Responsive Affirmation of Faith in the Holy Spirit

Minister: In the beginning the earth was without form and void, and the Spirit of God moved upon the face of the waters.

People: **We believe that God's spirit is ever at work to bring order out of chaos, life out of death, beauty out of ugliness, and meaning out of the shapeless events of daily life.**

Minister: God breathed into man's nostrils the breath of life, and man became a living soul.

People: **We believe that our true humanity depends on our continual response to God's spirit. Without him we are nothing; with him we are enabled to become creative, lively, and free.**

Minister: The Spirit of God came upon Saul, and he prophesied.

People: **We believe that the gift of prophecy, of clear sight and inspiring speech, belong to those who are open to the spirit of God.**

Minister: Come from the four winds, O breath, and breathe upon these slain that they may live.

People: **We believe in the spirit of vitality, energizing both men and nations, creating true community and genuine persons.**

Minister: And when the day of Pentecost was come, they were all with one accord in one place.

People: **We believe in the church of Jesus Christ, created by the spirit and empowered by its energy, and in the power of the people of God to witness to God's purpose and will.**

Minister: God hath not given us the spirit of fear but of power and of love and of a sound mind.

People: **We believe that God's spirit can deliver us from the fear that weakens the will, spoils love, and corrupts our minds, that in dependence on him we are made able for real choice, genuine love, and creative thought.**

AMEN.

A Responsive Affirmation of Faith in God's Will

Minister: Almighty God, whose thoughts are not as our thoughts and whose ways are not our ways, we seek to bring our lives into line with thine. We believe that thou hast made us for thyself, so that in joyful acceptance of thy will we grow into spiritual maturity and discover fulness of life.

People: **In thy will is our peace, in thy service is perfect freedom, and in thy presence is fullness of joy.**

Minister: We believe that thy will is made known to us in the words and deeds of Jesus Christ and that in him we are offered both the pattern and the power for living according to thy purpose.

People: **Looking unto Jesus, the author and finisher of faith, we will run the race that is set before us.**

Minister: We believe that thy will for us is health of body and mind, skill of brain and hand, the power to communicate ideas and to convey love, and the grace to impart health and truth to others.

People: **Putting away childish things, we will seek to grow up in all things unto the measure of the stature of the fullness of Christ.**

Minister: We believe that it is thy will that we live together in love and peace, each esteeming other better than himself and finding his life by losing it in thoughtful service for others.

People: **We are members one of another. Therefore, we renounce our false individualism and seek to become persons.**

Minister: We believe it is thy will that we stop drifting and act decisively, that we exercise responsibility for ourselves and others, and that we become fellowships of concern.

People: **A man shall be as a hiding place from the wind and as the shadow of a great rock in a weary land. So we believe; so we pray.**

Minister: We believe that thy will for us is also thy gift to us, that we are not left to our own resources, but that in thee there is power for every task.

People: **Jesus Christ is the wisdom and the power of God. In him, therefore, we reaffirm our trust and to him we pledge our troth.**

SECTION III

Meditations on Scripture

A Meditation on the Ten Commandments

And God spake all these words, saying, I am the Lord thy God, which have brought thee out of the land of Egypt, out of the house of bondage.

As we meditate on the commandments, let us remember that he who gave them was the Saviour-God who desired his people to escape from slavery into freedom. Let us listen to them in the spirit of him who said, "Thy statutes have been my songs in the house of my pilgrimage."

Thou shalt have no other gods before me. Thou shalt not bow down thyself to them, nor serve them.

Let us pray to be saved from idolatry, especially that modern form of it which consists of trying to serve one God with a fragmented self. If we have dissipated our loyalties or sold ourselves into slavery to unworthy causes or worshiped the creature more than the creator, let us pray to be forgiven.

Thou shalt not make unto thee any graven image.

Let us pray to be delivered from the temptation to

worship our ideas of God rather than God himself, from the sin of petrifying those ideas, and from all unwillingness to meet God in his contemporary claim and demand.

Thou shalt not take the name of the Lord thy God in vain; for the Lord will not hold him guiltless that taketh his name in vain.

Let us pray to be saved from careless talk about the Most High, from ascribing to him our human motives, from using him to further our own ends.

Remember the sabbath day, to keep it holy. Six days shalt thou labour, and do all thy work: but the seventh day is the sabbath of the Lord thy God.

Let us pray for a godly respect for work, for delight in sharing the creativity of God, for a sense of responsibility about craftsmanship, and for the ability to lay down that responsibility and rest. Let us pray for a healthy regard for the claims of the body, for the ability to let go the taut strings of the mind, and above all, for delight in contemplation and worship.

Honour thy father and thy mother: that thy days may be long upon the land which the Lord thy God giveth thee.

Let us pray for a healthy sense of tradition, for piety to the past, for respect and love for those who have nurtured and trained us, and for commitment to the family.

85

Thou shalt not kill.

Let us pray for reverence for life and for sensitiveness to all creation. Let us ask to be delivered from wanton destructiveness, from wasting the good gifts of God, from physical cruelty, and from that mental brutality that cripples life, that stunts human growth and murders the young shoots of idealism and effort.

Thou shalt not commit adultery.

Let us pray for a wholesome attitude to physical life, for a proper regard for human personality, for the ability to delight in beauty without wishing to possess it. Let us rebel against all that corrupts the relationship of men and women and against all that exploits the curiosity and growing awareness of the young.

Thou shalt not steal.

Let us pray to be saved from possessiveness about people and things, for the spirit that delights to share and spend and give, for freedom from acquisitiveness and greed. Let us dedicate ourselves to simplicity of life, to the discipline of desire, and to the fullest use of what we have.

Thou shalt not bear false witness against thy neighbour.

Let us pray for honesty in our relations with others, for scrupulous regard for the truth, for freedom from the sneer, the cynical leer, and the lifted eyebrow.

Let us seek for straightforward speech and generous judgment and the upbuilding of true social life.

Thou shalt not covet . . . any thing that is thy neighbour's.

Let us pray for contentment with what we have, for freedom from jealousy and envy, for dedication to the just society where covetousness is unnecessary, and where men have all things common in the fellowship of love.

AMEN.

A Meditation on Choice

See, I have set before thee this day life and good, and death and evil; . . . I have set before you life and death, blessing and cursing: therefore choose life, that both thou and thy seed may live: That thou mayest love the Lord thy God, and that thou mayest obey his voice, and that thou mayest cleave unto him: for he is thy life, and the length of thy days.

In this act of worship let us confront anew the necessity for choice, the call God makes upon us for decision and for the deliberate fronting of his will. And let us face the alternatives that present themselves to us.

Let us confess that we are wont to live by habit and custom, to avoid the pain of decision, to be carried on the tide of past choices and inherited convictions.

Let us pray to be forgiven for not wanting to decide, for resisting the choices that a new day and new problems present to us, and for trying to live on the accumulated choices of others.

Let us ask when we last confronted the present claims of God upon our lives, when we last decided from our own deep center to choose life and good, and when we last repudiated with all our being the false claims of death and evil.

I have set before thee this day life and death.

Let us pray for power to recognize what is life-enriching and what is life-diminishing, what attitudes, thoughts, and deeds bring us alive inside, and what attitudes, thoughts, and deeds create deadness within us.

Let us pray for power to shun what is negative in judgment, what is debilitating in emotion, what is weakening in imaginative reverie, and what is deadly in personal relationships. Let us commit ourselves anew to the Spirit that creates life, that recreates us inwardly, and that enhances life for those we meet.

I have set before you . . . blessing and cursing.

Let us pray for the ability to choose what graces and hallows life and to reject what frustrates and impoverishes it. Let us examine afresh those thoughts, words, and deeds that create havoc and bitterness, that we may loathe and repudiate them. Let us accept from Christ the power to do and say and think what enriches and blesses our own life and the lives we touch.

To this end may we give ourselves again to the love of God that he may give himself to us.

AMEN.

A Meditation on the 103rd Psalm

Bless the Lord, O my soul: and all that is within me, bless his holy name.

All that is within me! Let us try to say that honestly—with body as well as with mind, with our senses as well as with the soul, with intellect as well as with our will, with imagination as well as with reason.

Let us ask for forgiveness for our one-sided worship, for being more spiritual than God, for keeping our bodies out of our prayers, for our emotional immaturity and unevangelized imaginations.

Let us lift up our whole being, body, mind, and spirit in one united act of worship.

Breathe on me, breath of God, until this *earthly* part of me
Glows with thy fire divine.

All that is within me! Let us try to say that practically—with work as well as with prayer, with play as well as with labor, with activity as well as with rest, with opposition as well as with co-operation.

Let us ask forgiveness for departmentalizing life, for serving God in limited areas, for asking his blessing on what we have already decided is good, for neglecting to acknowledge his Lordship over all life.

Let us seek to serve him in political responsibility, in artistic discrimination, in creative integrity, and in the width and depth of our community involvement.

Take my *mind,* that I may think thy thoughts after thee.
Suffuse and possess my *spirit* that it may touch thy life
And be touched by it.

All that is within me! Let us try to say that as churchmen—with gratitude for tradition as well as daring experiment, with concern for our local fellowship and commitment to the world church, with reverence for the house of God and for the secular world, with love for the brethren, and with yearning for those who are without.

Let us ask forgiveness if we have made denominationalism a stone of stumbling, if we have cherished the folk we know and love and agree with and isolated ourselves from the outsider, and if we have equated religion with what we do in church.

Let us pray that we may bless God by taking the church to the world and by bringing the world into the church, by making our discipleship secular, and by offering the riches of our denominational life as a contribution to the one Church.

AMEN.

A Meditation on the Beatitudes

In our prayer time this morning let us recall, and meditate upon, the words of Jesus to his disciples.

Jesus said: Blessed are the poor in spirit: for theirs is the kingdom of heaven.

Let us thank God that the riches of life lie open to us, without money and without price, that the kingdom of heaven breaks in upon us in the experience of friendship and love, in shared conversation and common tasks, in response to earth's beauty, and as we wrestle for truth and integrity.

Let us confess, however, that because we have been arrogant in spirit, the kingdom has often remained closed to us. We have tried to bully life, to exploit it instead of loving and appreciating it, to own it rather than to enjoy it as a free gift. And let us ask to be delivered from all ugly possessiveness that strives to create a private heaven or to imprison people within our small circle.

Jesus said: Blessed are they that mourn: for they shall be comforted.

Let us remember that those who have mourned in the spirit of Jesus, who have been inwardly distressed by the sorrow and evil around them, have found the comfort of his spirit. As they identified themselves with the helpless and dispossessed, they grew under the burdens they assumed; they experienced a fellowship with him that the selfish and self-occupied can never know.

If we have sought comfort on easier terms than this, let us ask forgiveness. Let us pray to be delivered from the luxury of self-pity and from seeking sympathy when we have no intention of giving it.

92

Jesus said: Blessed are the meek: for they shall inherit the earth.

Let us remind ourselves that the world belongs to those who have no designs upon it and who, therefore, own things though they do not possess them. The good earth yields its fruit to those who respect its rights; truth is found by those who are willing to be the servants of truth; beauty discovers herself to those who are patient and reverent; goodness is given to those who seek not their own righteousness but the Kingdom of God.

And let us pray for pardon if we have confused meekness with weakness. Let us ask for the strength that permits us to cast self aside.

Jesus said: Blessed are they which hunger and thirst after righteousness: for they shall be filled.

Let us thank God for divine discontent, for the alarmed conscience, and the conviction of sin, which prove that we are still sensitive to his spirit. Let us ask to be rescued from complacency and from satisfaction with yesterday's achievements and insights and from evading duties and tasks that would expose our need of fresh resources.

But, lest we mistake the restless search for novelty for the true search for God, let us ask him to feed our souls upon the abiding Word made flesh in Jesus Christ our Lord.

And let us ask to be delivered from seeking fulfillment on a low level, from trying to solve the problems of the spirit on the plane of the flesh, from the attempt to dull the appetite for spiritual things by filling our lives with material satisfactions and ephemeral pleasures.

Jesus said: Blessed are the merciful: for they shall obtain mercy.

Let us give thanks for the divine mercy that meets our sin with forgiveness and for the human mercy that lifts us up when we fall. Our little lives are held in a context of grace; we receive far more than we give and are sustained day by day by the readiness of others to believe in us and to trust us.

Let us ask to be rebuked when we fail in mercy to others or try to withhold mercy in order to assert our superiority, or when we confuse mercy with indifference and live by the principle, "Blessed are the easy-going, for they shall be let off."

Jesus said: Blessed are the pure in heart: for they shall see God.

Let us thank God that moral perfection is not expected of us, or we should be undone. "Purity of heart is to will one thing," to focus life on him and on his Kingdom. Fellowship with him and service in his kingdom purifies life, cleanses the windows of the soul, burns up the dross of the heart.

Let us recall the words of our Master: "This is life eternal, that they might know thee," that we may make all of life a sharing of his love and an experience of his presence.

Let us ask to be saved from thinking that we can know anyone, much less God, if we are unwilling to be real and open.

Jesus said: Blessed are the peacemakers: for they shall be called the children of God.

Let us give thanks for the makers of peace, for the ministers of reconciliation who create bridges across the chasms of misunderstanding, and especially for people who have created peace in our lives by reconciling us to our lot, by saving us from bitterness and resentment, by restoring us to fellowship with others. Verily, they are the children of God to us!

Let us pray to be enlisted among their number, to offer ourselves anew to God for his use. To this end let us ask for the spirit of God to sweeten our bitter-thoughted hearts and to endow us with the love that outwears all malice and hate.

Jesus said: Blessed are they which are persecuted for righteousness' sake: for theirs is the kingdom of heaven.

Let us remember what we owe to the witnesses and martyrs of bygone days, to those who were not ashamed to confess the Lordship of Christ in an evil day.

Let us ask for strength to accept persecution, though not to seek it. Let us ask for grace to speak the truth in love, to be silent when speech would be an evasion, to act always with a sense of stewardship, placing the results in the hand of God. And may our ultimate aim be the spread of the kingdom of love and joy and peace, not our own justification.

AMEN.

A Meditation on the Hymn of Love

Though I speak with the tongues of men and of angels, and have not charity, I am become as sounding brass, or a tinkling cymbal.

Let us pray to be delivered from all empty rhetoric, all cheap talk, all words without love.

If we have tried to solve problems by coining phrases or talked simply to show off, or bullied people into submission with a flow of argument, let us ask to be forgiven.

Let us pray to be given the gift of real speech—conversation that builds men up, that addresses men as men and not as adversaries, that is sensitive to their personal needs and hopes and fears.

And though I have the gift of prophecy, and understand all mysteries, and all knowlege; and though I have all faith, so that I could remove mountains, and have not charity, I am nothing.

Let us pray to be delivered from soulless thinking, from intellectual Pharisaism, and from devotion to causes unaccompanied by love of people.

If we have alienated people by intellectual arrogance or brushed aside their feelings with clever arguments or loved humanity in the abstract more than we loved particular men and women, let us ask to be forgiven.

Let us pray for minds suffused with tenderness, for thinking that is informed by pasion and sympathy.

And though I bestow all my goods to feed the poor, and though I give my body to be burned, and have not charity, it profiteth me nothing.

Let us pray to be delivered from patronizing people, from regarding them as "cases," and from lavishing upon them everything but love.

If we have made people paupers by our gifts or chained them to ourselves in helpless dependence or "sacrificed" ourselves for them ostentatiously, let us pray to be forgiven.

Let us pray for true charity that delights in giving and makes the gift an expression of love, and for true sacrifice that permits and encourages others to be themselves.

Charity suffereth long, and is kind.

Let us pray to be delivered from the desire for quick results, from forcing the pace, from impatience, and from unrequited love that turns to anger and resentment.

Charity envieth not.

Let us pray for largeness of spirit and for love that delights in the victories of others and knows the grace of congratulating and commending them.

Charity vaunteth not itself, is not puffed up.

Let us pray for deliverance from self-centeredness, for the ability to work without wanting public recognition, and for freedom from pride in our own achievements.

Doth not behave itself unseemly, seeketh not her own, is not easily provoked.

Let us pray for the grace to give gracefully, to confer favors without vulgarity, to ask nothing in return save the spread of Christ's kingdom, and for power to remain undisturbed by disappointment.

Thinketh no evil; rejoiceth not in iniquity, but rejoiceth in the truth.

Let us pray to be kept free of suspicion, to resist the temptation to say "I told you so," and for love that delights when truth and goodness and beauty prevail.

Beareth all things, believeth all things, hopeth all things, endureth all things.

Let us pray for confidence in the spirit of God, for the faith to see him at work in human aspiration and repentance, and for patient continuance in friendship and hope.

Charity never faileth.

Let us pray for grace to continue when things go wrong, to forgive until seventy times seven, to lift up the fallen and begin again, and to enter into the meaning of bearing Christ's cross.

AMEN.

A Meditation on the Words of Jesus to His Disciples

In this act of worship let us recall the commissions Jesus laid upon his disciples, and let us face them anew for our own time.

Ye are the salt of the earth.
Ye are the light of the world. . . . Let your light so
  shine.
The kingdom of heaven is like unto leaven.

Let us pray:

Almighty God, we would come face to face this day with the gracious imperatives of Jesus Christ, our Master; help us to accept them with quiet confidence and grateful responsibility.

1. Through him God is calling us to be the light of the world. Let us confess with shame that all too often we have been part of its darkness, obscuring issues rather than clarifying them, plunging men into confusion, and making choices difficult. By our own feeble flame that is all we can do, it seems.

Let us ask Jesus Christ, who is the light that lighteth every man coming into the world, to suffuse our lives with the light of his spirit, that, whether we speak or whether we keep silent, our whole being might illumine life for others, might shed light upon the path of those who are hesitant and confused, and point men to the light that is eternal and unchanging.

"Lord, I am praying to be lighted from within, not only to hold a candle in my hand." [1]

2. We believe that God is calling us to be the salt

[1] Rabindranath Tagore.

100

of the earth. Let us confess with shame that we have often been part of the world's corruption, not of its health, that we have again and again been flavorless and without power to bring out the flavor in others.

Let us ask for help to live so intimately "in Christ" that our very presence among men might disinfect the atmosphere and save the world from going rotten. Whoever else profits by lies, may we be truthful; whoever else finds happiness in evasion, compromise, and vapidity, let us strive to be men and women of integrity.

And let us ask that, like salt, we might bring out the best in other people; may we so live that others might find it easier to be their genuine selves.

3. We believe that we are called to be leaven within the lump. Let us repent if we have been part of the heavy, doughy mass, without power to quicken and enliven life for others, and if our conversation has been without inspiration or our deeds have not lifted men to new heights.

Let us pray to be so possessed by the spirit of Christ that we might bring ferment into lives that have grown dull and stodgy, that our Christ-given zest for living might give zest to those who are bored and aimless, that our joy in the service of Christ might win men for the adventure of living in his creative service.

AMEN.

A Meditation on Being Lost and Found

The Son of man is come to seek and to save that which was lost.

Let us give thanks that we are not left to our own devices, that we live our human lives in a context of grace, that many hands go out to rescue us from ourselves, that we are surrounded by undeserved trust and forgiveness and love.

Let us give thanks, above all, that Jesus Christ is the great seeker, that we can never put ourselves outside his care and his passion for our salvation.

Let us remember that he seeks to save us from waste, from triviality, from inertia, from indecision, as well as from sin and fear. So let us examine ourselves in the light of his words.

I have found my sheep which was lost.

Let us pray to be delivered from aimlessness and drift.

If we have sinned through want of direction, through following the impulse of the moment, or through shortsighted desire for temporary satisfaction, let us pray to be rescued and forgiven and restored.

Let us pray for long views and worthy ends, for the ability to distinguish between what is permanent

102

and what is passing, and for strength to dedicate ourselves to ultimate goals.

I have found the piece which I had lost.

Let us pray to be saved from disuse, from falling out of circulation, and from slipping out of the Owner's hand.

If we have sinned through careless living or allowed ourselves to rust unused or failed to take part in the commerce of human relationships, let us ask to be rescued, restored, and made serviceable.

Let us pray that our lives might be profitable in the interests of the kingdom of God.

And let us pray for all who sin through the carelessness of other people, for those who are held in no grasp of love, and for those who are permitted no opportunities of service. Let us rebel against all that tarnishes the brightness of youth, that makes no use of youth's idealism and talents, and that exploits the ability of youth for wasteful ends.

This my son was lost, and is found.

Let us pray to be redeemed from rebellion against the Father's house and from detachment from the human family.

If we have sinned through deliberate choice or because we craved excitement and false independence or because we took love and security and service for granted, let us pray to be forgiven and reclaimed for the Father's house.

Let us pray for growth from individualism to personality, from isolation to community, and from wrong-headed independence to grateful co-operation with the Creator of our lives.

And let us commit ourselves to the upbuilding of the human family and to the creation of a world where there is more excitement in belonging than in separation.

Bring forth the best robe, and put it on him; and put a ring on his hand, and shoes on his feet.

Let us rejoice in the promise of Christ.

Let us forego all vain regrets, all self-punishing remorse, and let us allow ourselves to be forgiven.

In freedom from self-righteousness let us seek to share the forgiveness of God with others, to clothe them in the robe of sonship, and to redeem them from penury and want, both material and spiritual.

AMEN.

A Meditation on Christian Rest

Let us make our prayer time this morning a meditation on the gracious invitation of Jesus Christ.

Come unto me, all ye that labour and are heavy laden, and I will give you rest. Take my yoke upon you, and learn of me; for I am meek and lowly in heart: and ye shall find rest unto your souls. For my yoke is easy, and my burden is light.

Come unto me, all ye that labour and are heavy laden.

In the presence of Jesus Christ let us ask what has caused our fatigue and listlessness. Have we wearied ourselves in evading him? Have we squandered psychic energy in bypassing life's responsibilities, in hesitation and indecision, in restless activity for the sake of activity?

Let us seek the rest that comes from singleminded devotion and from openness to the resources of the kingdom of Christ.

Take my yoke upon you, and learn of me.

Let us ask whether we are seeking rest or only "peace and quiet." Are we genuinely wanting the poise and strength that comes from commitment to a great cause, a great person?

Are we uneasily yoked to many partners, unstable in our loyalties, fickle in our trust?

Are we unwilling to bear the yoke because we are falsely independent or foolishly proud?

Let us ask to recognize the true dignity of life—its glad acceptance of unbought grace and undeserved love.

My yoke is easy, and my burden is light.

Let us pray to be delivered from seeking to be God.

Let us ask to be rescued from trying to do everything in our own strength, from being martyrs to duty, from turning religion into drudgery, and from fearing to accept help from God.

Let us seek our place within the kingdom of his Son, that the powers of that kingdom might become available to us. Let us pray for enlistment in that service which is perfect freedom, for surrender to that will in which is our peace, and for fellowship with him in whose presence there is fullness of joy.

> God strengthen me to bear myself;
> That heaviest weight of all to bear,
> Inalienable weight of care.
>
> .   .   .   .
>
> God harden me against myself,
> This coward with pathetic voice
> Who craves for ease, and rest, and joys:
>
> Myself, arch-traitor to myself;
> My hollowest friend, my deadliest foe,
> My clog whatever road I go.

Yet One there is can curb myself,
Can roll the strangling load from me,
Break off the yoke and set me free.[2]

A Meditation on the Spirit of Truth

*When he [the Spirit of Truth] is come, he will re-
prove the world of sin, and of righteousness, and of
judgment.*

As we meditate upon these words, let us pray to be
open to the Spirit of Truth, that we might be led
out of partial insights into fulness of truth and out of
error into reality.

He will reprove the world of sin.

The world has its own ideas about sin.
The man of the world thinks sin is being found out.
The child thinks sin is wanting his own way.
The idealist thinks sin is failure to live up to his
own high standards.

[2] Christina Rossetti, "The Battle Within."
107

The religious man thinks sin is breaking the law of God.

For many of us sin is a messy muddle of all these.

Jesus said: *He will reprove the world . . . of sin, because they believe not on me.*

The sin behind all sins is failure to take God at his word. Let us search our ways and ask whether we accept or resist what God has done for us in Christ; let us ask if this fundamental failure lies at the root of our lovelessness, our fear, our want of charity, our grasping for earthly possessions.

He will reprove the world of . . . righteousness.

The world has its own ideas about righteousness.

Men are obsessed with righteousness—save the children, help the refugees, improve the schools, ban the atom tests, work for peace, promote integration! It recognizes responsibility, is worried about it, and cannot compass it.

Jesus said: *He will reprove the world . . . of righteousness, because I go to my Father, and ye see me no more.*

Let us ask whether we have been striving for righteousness in our own strength or in God's.

Is our righteousness, resurrection righteousness, the glad acceptance of divine resources offered to us through Jesus Christ?

Do we want righteousness or peace and quiet?

He will reprove the world . . . of judgment.

The world has its own ideas about judgment.

It fears that the threat of war may be a judgment on its greed and rapacity. It thinks that judgment is a punishment for sin.

It fears judgment and seeks to avoid it.

Jesus said: *He will reprove the world . . . of judgment, because the prince of this world is judged.*

Should we not welcome judgment, since it is Christ's exposure in mercy? In avoiding judgment, are we not running away from our true humanity? Is not man always under judgment? Is not this the permanent crisis of man—to stand under the saving judgment of Jesus the Christ.

AMEN.

A Meditation on the Power of the Keys

I will give unto thee the keys of the kingdom of heaven: and whatsoever thou shalt bind on earth shall be bound in heaven: and whatsoever thou shalt loose on earth shall be loosed in heaven.

Let us remember that God has thrust great responsibilities upon us. Even the humblest of us are capable of creating heaven or hell for someone.

With the key of love we may open life up; with the key of unforgiving resentment and hate we may shut men in upon themselves.

Let us pray for pardon if we have brought discouragement and blight upon life through our unwillingness to forgive, if we have imprisoned men within their failures and deepened their feeling of despair.

Let us ask for the power to set men free by our attitude of trust and confidence in them, by sharing with them the forgiveness that has come to us in Christ, and by creating openings of service and friendship for them.

Let us remember that the power of the keys is ours whether we want it or not; it already resides in our hands. But the power of the kingdom of heaven is given to those who make the acknowledgment of God in Christ, as Peter and the disciples did. Let us, therefore, affirm anew, from the deep center of our lives, that in Jesus of Nazareth we see and acknowledge God's Christ and are henceforth resolved to organize our lives around him.

Let us recall that the power of the keys was given to Peter and the others, who constituted the first Christian fellowship, and so let us realize anew the meaning of the Church. Let us ask if our church fellowship is liberating men and introducing them to the glorious liberty of the children of God or shutting men in upon themselves. Let us pray for a fellowship capable of "opening the kingdom to all believers."

The risen Christ said:

I am he that liveth, and was dead; and, behold, I am alive for evermore, Amen; and have the keys of hell and of death.

Let us reaffirm our faith in the power of the living Christ, who, through his death and resurrection, is able again and again to redeem us from sin and fear. In his strength may we recover the power of the keys, even when we have lost it, and so make daily conquests over hell and death.

Let us pray that the Church may evermore be the Church of which he is the Head and recreator.

Let us pray that she may open doors between men and men, between alien cultures and differing faiths, and between land and land.

AMEN.

A Meditation on Newness of Life

If any man be in Christ, he is a new creature: old things are passed away; behold, all things are become new.

Let us rejoice in the power of Christ to recreate our manhood, to give us a new status before God, to bring forth powers we never suspected within ourselves, and to redeem us from the drag of the past.

Let us ask forgiveness if we have preferred the familiarity of the old: old ways, old thoughts, old relationships, and old roads to tread in.

Let us meditate afresh upon the newness of Christ's life, the freshness of each day's repose to the Father's love and to the world's need, the newness of his grasp of truth, the newness of his surrender to love.

Let us ask that we may be made new now in this latest encounter with his life and love.

Jesus said: *Behold, I make all things new.*

Let us give thanks that the living Christ makes *all* things new, that he takes the stale stuff of daily life— its worn routine, its shabby tiredness—and gives it vitality and freshness, that he is able to show us new sights to see, new thoughts to think, new tasks to essay, that he makes unfamiliar what was commonplace and gives us new eyes to see people, things, and the hand of God in life.

Let us pray for his power to save us from seeking what is novel, that we might turn with zest to experience the old in a new way.

Jesus said: *Every scribe which is instructed unto the kingdom of heaven is like unto a man that is an householder, which bringeth forth out of his treasure things new and old.*

Let us pray so to be instructed in the kingdom of God that we also might have the power to bring forth things new and old, to communicate with those whose thoughts are in the past, to share with those whose eyes are on the future, to reconcile in one fellowship the conservatives and the radicals, and to make both at home within the kingdom of love.

Jesus said: *A new commandment I give unto you, That ye love one another; as I have loved you, that ye also love one another. By this shall all men know that ye are my disciples, if ye have love one to another.*

Let us place ourselves anew into the living hands of Christ and seek to embody and express his love.

Let us look with new eyes upon the faces of our fellow men that we may see them with the compassion of Christ; let us learn that every situation is a new one when we see God in it; let us trust in the power of Christ's crucified and risen life to cleanse and renew our love for one another.

O come, let us sing a new song unto the Lord!

AMEN.

A Meditation on Non-Conformity and Transformation

I beseech you therefore, brethren, by the mercies of God, that ye present your bodies a living sacrifice, holy, acceptable unto God, which is your reasonable service. And be not conformed to this world: but be ye transformed by the renewing of your mind, that ye may prove what is that good, and acceptable, and perfect, will of God.

Be not conformed to this world.

Let us pray to be saved from adjusting ourselves to the world instead of rebelling against it.

Let us ask to be forgiven if we have esteemed the praise of men more than the favor of God, if we have worked only with an eye to applause and acceptance by society, if we have reckoned success by worldly standards, and if we have striven to efface ourselves in the mass to escape discomfort and decision.

Let us reunite ourselves with Christ, who loved the world and yet never succumbed to it, whose love was a thrust of revolt against all that was tame and conformist, and who was the Pioneer of Life, blazing a trail for us lesser men.

Let us commit ourselves anew to the standards and values of the kingdom of God, offering ourselves as instruments and agents of that kingdom. Let us pray to be transformers of thought, boldly carrying the

114

mind of Christ into all our relationships; let us pray to be transformers of feeling, making sensitive the emotions of men to what is lovely and of good report; let us pray to be transformers of judgment, giving men a new standard of measurement through Jesus Christ.

Whom he did foreknow, he also did predestinate to be conformed to the image of his Son, that he might be the firstborn among many brethren.

Let us pray that Christ might be born in us, displacing the old life of egotism and fear with his life of confident joy and swift obedience; let us pray for the renewing of our minds that we might have that mind in us which was also in Christ Jesus, who, being in the form of God, counted it not a prize to be snatched at to be on an equality with God but made himself of no reputation.

AMEN.

Meditations on Jesus Christ

The Bread of Life

Let us give thanks for Jesus Christ, who is the Staff of Life, its plain wholesome fare building up our manhood and strengthening every natural endowment.

Let us repent if we turn to him only as a desperate remedy, as medicine for our sickness, not realizing that he is the Lord of all good life, without whom we cannot be truly human.

Let us give thanks that he satisfies every hunger of the soul, and that he fulfills every legitimate demand of body, mind, and spirit.

Let us confess with shame that we have often ignored him because we have lost our appetite for plain food, because we have dulled the edge of hunger on sweetmeats and substitutes, esteeming the sensational and exceptional better than the satisfying and ordinary.

Let us give thanks that in Christ we find not only bread to eat but bread to share, that he has taught us to find the durable satisfactions of life in fellowship and service.

Let us ask forgiveness for every attempt to hoard the good things of life, to use possessions to enhance prestige or find security rather than to relate ourselves more fully to our fellow men.

Let us give thanks that in Christ we find the meaning of our daily bread and the right use of it. Bread is material, but what we do with it is spiritual. Let us aim to see in it the symbol of our dependence upon God and upon one another, a means of grace.

Let us pray to be saved from eating our bread alone.

Let us ask pardon for eating bread without thankfulness or for using it to our brother's impoverishment or for building up physical strength without spiritual growth.

Let us give thanks that bread can become sacramental, since Jesus took bread at the table of fellowship in the Upper Room and said, "Do this in remembrance of me." So every common meal and every occasion of human fellowship may become a celebration of our life in Christ.

Let us confess with shame that we have often abused and misused the gifts of God; we have lost sight of him where we should have discovered him, in the duties and opportunities of everyday. We have used his good gifts to our own hurt, and to the hurt of his kingdom.

O Jesus Christ, who art the nourishment upon which we feed, enable us to reach out for thee and take thee.

AMEN.

The Light of the World

I am the light of the world.

It was an astonishing claim to make! The great lamps of Jewish religion and the brilliant light of Greece had shed all the light that was required. Yet many sat in darkness and in the shadow of death.

However loudly Socrates cried, "Know thyself," they still remained enigmas and strangers to themselves —till he came who revealed the secrets of many hearts. Though Israel thundered, "It is written," the words conveyed little light—till he came who shed the light of his life upon the book.

Let us stand where the light of his life and death and resurrection shines into the darkness of our lives, till his words search and expose the hollowness of our words and his purity judges our sin.

We stand in our own light and wonder why it is dark; let us turn and face him whose light both reveals and heals.

He that followeth me shall not walk in darkness, but shall have the light of life.

The light is light to walk in. Let us ask to be saved from merely intellectual curiosity. As men long ago discovered in Christ the path they should tread and found life growing clearer and finer as they tread it, so let us highly resolve to walk by the light we have. Let us pray, "One step enough for me," but let us take that step in full assurance of faith that he is able.

In him was life; and the life was the light of men.

The life was the light! The perfect humanity of Jesus illumines the meaning of human life. The sacrifice of his cross reveals the strategy of Christian living. The empty tomb assures us of victory. All that Jesus was sheds light on our existence. His baptism summons us to find joy in identification with others; his temptation reveals the meaning of our struggles.

Let us, who are caricatures of true human beings, find the wholeness of our humanity in the life that is life indeed.

For God, who commanded the light to shine out of darkness, hath shined in our hearts, to give the light of the knowledge of the glory of God in the face of Jesus Christ.

Let us rejoice that in the face of Christ we see the Divine Face, that we know the heart of God, and that he has taken the initiative in enlightening us. As we love him because he first loved us, so we know him because he has chosen to reveal himself. So we are rescued from our uncertain subjectivism, from our wayward feelings; the Lord himself hath spoken unto us.

Ye are the light of the world. . . . Let your light so shine before men, that they may see your good works, and glorify your Father which is in heaven.

Let us humbly and gratefully accept the commission that is laid upon us. Like light that does not call attention to itself but illumines all objects upon which it falls, so let us live that men understand themselves better because of us, that they grow surer of the meaning and purpose of life, and that they learn to trust the love and mercy of God.

AMEN.

The Door

I am the door.

We recall, in this act of meditation, how Jesus of Nazareth liberated men in the days of his flesh. Through the breach he made in the blank wall of their existence, they glimpsed new horizons and saw the spacious beauty of the Father's world. Because of him men lost their provincialism and became citizens of a better country; their eyes were opened to new frontiers; they dared to step out of their prisons into freedom.

Let us confess that we have become so accustomed to the safety of small quarters and little views that the door he opens to us sometimes frightens rather than allures us; we have grown to love the walls that hem us in.

Let us ask for courage to pass through the gateway he presents to us, to take him at his word as he beckons us to new adventures of understanding and conquest.

By me if any man enter in, he shall be saved, and shall go in and out, and find pasture.

To many who were strangers to themselves, Christ has been the door to self-knowledge; through him they have taken possession of their own lives. To many who lived on the outskirts of existence, he has been an introduction to its centralities, has opened up the treasures they never suspected within things they took for granted—love and friendship, work and leisure.

Let us confess that we have lacked the will to dig deep, to take full possession of ourselves, to enter into the full possibilities of the day's tasks, to discover the full riches of real personal encounter.

Let us ponder afresh the roads we have feared to take, the new continents of thought and experience we have not dared to enter, and let us ask for courage to be led, through Christ, into new fields of service and into new triumphs of grace.

Behold, I have set before thee an open door, and no man can shut it.

Let us rejoice that the Living Christ is still the door to growth and fulfillment, and that no earthly power can frustrate the Christian future. The way forward for humanity is towards Christ, not away from him.

Let us ask to be saved from capitulating to outward threats, from being cowed by the seeming victories of principalities and powers.

Behold, I stand at the door, and knock.

Let us rejoice that we are not left to our own devices, that the Living Christ seeks to enter our lives and lead us out from bondage into freedom. Where we have no courage to enter his door, he stands at our door, ever inviting us to come forth and travel with him.

Let us pray to give heed to his voice, to repent of our stubborn fear and timidity.

For a great door and effectual is opened unto me, and there are many adversaries.

Emboldened and empowered by Christ, his servants in every age have found doors opening before them. The very darkness and hostility they encountered provided them with an opportunity for witness and service.

Let us ask to see the open doors of our generation —the promise within the peril, the invitation to evangelism within the chaos of our time, the hidden appeal within the desperation of men. Let us enter in the strength of the Lord and take possession. Let us rejoice that we are counted worthy to live in a time of upheaval, knowing that man's extremity is God's opportunity.

AMEN.

The Good Shepherd

I am the good shepherd: the good shepherd giveth his life for the sheep.

Being human, we all need good leadership and guidance. Let us seek to learn the difference between leaders who exploit their followers and leaders who serve them. Let us thank God for the leadership of Jesus Christ, who does not use his power for self-expression or to enhance his own prestige. The Good Shepherd gives his life for the sheep. Where others

122

give counsel, good advice, and help, he gives himself.

But great leadership demands great following; let us ask whether we are prepared to give it.

I am the good shepherd, and know my sheep, and am known of mine.

If it humiliates us to be regarded as sheep, let us candidly recall how sheepish we have often been, how conformist in our behavior, how conventional in our thought, how panic-stricken to find ourselves alone without the support of the crowd.

Let us rejoice that, knowing our weakness, Jesus Christ seeks to win us for ourselves. He knows us by name, as persons not as ciphers, and ever seeks to gain from us a truly personal response.

And other sheep I have, which are not of this fold: them also I must bring, and they shall hear my voice; and there shall be one fold, and one shepherd.

Let us rejoice that Christ is weaning us from collectivity to community. As members of his Church, let us test our churchmanship by his words; let us ask whether we are open or closed; let us seek to make the hearing and obeying of his voice the true test of discipleship; let us pray for the true unity of the Church.

He that is an hireling, . . . whose own the sheep are not, . . . fleeth: . . . because he is an hireling, and careth not for the sheep.

In discharging our responsibility as undershepherds, let us ask how deeply we are committed to the sheep. If we are hireling shepherds, always seeking our own advantage or our own growth, let us ask forgiveness. Let us test our church life by the manner in which we care; let us seek to put our caring into practice.

I am come that they might have life, and that they might have it more abundantly.

Let us be sure that it is life we want and not security.

AMEN.

The Way, the Truth, and the Life

I am the way, the truth, and the life.

I am the way. Let us ask whether we are seeking a path or a goal. Have we succumbed to the lure of false finalities, finished solutions, easy answers? Do we want to be out on the road with Christ?

Let us seek wisdom to distinguish between the inn at the side of the road and the Father's house, lest we mistake the temporary halt for the ultimate end. If Christ is the way, the end of life is fellowship with God, and that can never be a final achievement.

I am the truth. Let us ask whether we want the disturbing encounter with truth—or the satisfaction of knowing the answers?

Where is the wisdom we have lost in knowledge?
Where is the knowledge we have lost in information?

If Christ is the truth, can we ever come to the end of it; can we ever hope to know it without relating ourselves in serious commitment to him? If truth is personal, can we go on evading real personal encounter with others?

Let us ask to be forgiven for resisting the claims of truth, for seeking to exploit it in our own interests instead of humbly seeking to be used by it.

I am the life. Do we love life enough to want more of it, to want it in abundance? Let us be honest about our fear of life, our secret hatred of it, our vain attempts to diminish it, to kill time, to damp down the fires of vitality. Let us enlist among those who fight against all that crushes life, that dehumanizes and defeats people, that saps vitality, that simply uses energy without replacing it.

AMEN.

The Resurrection and the Life

Jesus said . . . I am the resurrection, and the life: he that believeth in me, though he were dead, yet shall he live: And whosoever liveth and believeth in me shall never die.

Let us give thanks that Christ delivers us from the deadness of habit and custom. Though we are wrapped in the graveclothes of past failures and despairs, he leads us out of the tomb into the sunlight of hope.

Let us give thanks that when we are dead in trespasses and sins, his voice has power to call us forth. Where sin abounds his grace much more abounds.

Let us give thanks that our passing days may be shot through and through with eternity and saved from triviality and aimlessness.

Let us give thanks that in Christ our lives are beyond the reach of time; its wear and tear cannot diminish us.

Let us give thanks that the death of the body is not the end of us. Through the resurrection of Jesus Christ we enter through the door of his victory into further fellowship with God, the Eternal One.

Because Christ lives, we live also. He brings alive all that is moribund in us, quickens every wasting energy, vitalizes every drooping hope.

Of us, too, may it be said, "Because they live, others live also." May our Christian zest and eagerness awaken what is dull and slumbering in other people; may we be so alive to beauty, truth, and goodness that others may come awake to them also; may we live so richly in God that others may seek and find him.

O Jesus Christ, who broke the power of death because thou couldst not be holden of it, break the chains that bind us to the deadly past and quicken our mortal bodies that they might become carriers of eternal life.

AMEN.

SECTION IV

Pastoral Prayers
Based on
The Words of Jesus

A Prayer for First Things First

Jesus said: *Seek ye first the kingdom of God.*

Almighty God, we come to stand this day under the judgment of thy Word. In Jesus Christ thou hast bidden us seek first the kingdom of God, and we are convicted of divided loyalties and uncertain aims. We have not put first things first but have idolized the means and forgotten the ends; we have striven for reputation and forgotten character; we have worked for approval and not for integrity. Above all we have struggled to rule instead of to serve, to set up our petty kingdoms in isolation from thy kingdom of joy and love and peace.

Forgive us if we have made a kingdom of our homes, our careers, our public life, our domestic life, if we have sought plenitude and security in possessions, titles, honors, self-regard. Grant that we may see afresh that our little kingdoms are forever unsafe and unsure till they are founded in thine.

Thou hast called us to be a kingdom of priests; teach us to recover for our time the priesthood of all believers. In a world that is ruled by individualism, help us to be persons; in a day when men seek their own, help us to spend and share and give; in a day when men scramble for the glittering prizes of life, help us to compete for the lowest place, for the opportunities of service and the privilege of reconciliation.

Help us to welcome the inbreak of thy Kingdom into our daily lives; may we so work and think and act that our deeds and words may permit thee to reveal and give thyself to men and encourage men to give themselves to thee.

Help us, as a church, to pray "thy Kingdom come," lest we become ingrowing and esteem the institution more than the mission. And may we so live as churchmen, in the full life of our time, that we might bring to birth the latent Church within every human group and every secular society.

O Jesus Christ, who, by undergoing the sharpness of death, didst open the Kingdom of heaven to all believers, draw us into its joyful servitude; replenish our poverty with its abundant riches.

And this we ask for thy name's sake.

AMEN.

A Prayer to Abstain from Judging

Jesus said: *Judge not, that ye be not judged.*

O God, our heavenly Father, who shinest upon the evil and the good and sendest thy rain on the just and the unjust, forgive us our hasty discrimination.

Forgive us if we label men, if we substitute slogans for thought and estimate our fellows without first-hand knowledge of them. Forgive us when we fail to see people because we are preoccupied with abstractions like "principles" and "justice" and "tradition." Forgive us when we are more intent on being right than on being reconciled. Forgive us, too, when we refrain from judgment for the wrong reasons—through fear of recrimination or lack of sensitiveness.

May it become our passion, as it is thine, to enter into fellowship with men, to win men not for our party labels but for the truth. Save us when we isolate ourselves in self-righteousness, when we prefer to win an argument than to make a friend, and when we exalt order and safety over the good of the human person.

Lord, we are set down in a world where judgment is passed every day, where men are forced to pass sentence, to mete out punishment, and to administer the law. Help us to work and pray for redemption rather than recrimination, to shape a society where men are won for goodness rather than used as scape-goats, and where vindictiveness is curbed by love. Help us to sympathize with those who are compelled to do the disagreeable work of correction, while working always for the increase of thy kingdom of forgiving grace.

As thou hast called us into the fellowship of the Redeemed, so help us as church members to maintain a church where all are welcome, and where all men are met with openness and trust. Yet save us from shallow sentimentality or unreal romanticism; help us to see in men the ones for whom Christ died and to share his love for them.

And these things we ask for his name's sake.

AMEN.

A Prayer for Following Jesus

Jesus said: *Follow me.*

O God, whose son Jesus of Nazareth recruited men in the days of his flesh, we who live amid the complexities of the modern age still feel the pull of his command. But we are beset by many doubts and the fear of seeming to oversimplify life. The roots of our life are deeply entwined with the lives of others; we cannot tear ourselves away from family and civic commitments; we are legitimately bound to our children and their future.

Teach us to obey thee within the family, to follow thy Son in filial devotion, to accept as he did the responsibilities of our domestic ties. Teach us to follow him where he accepted life's restrictions and fulfilled them by perfect obedience. Teach us to obey before we rebel and to serve before we sever; yet make us ever ready to break with loyalties that cripple our loyalty to thee.

As men of the modern age we are also men who know the crucified and risen Lord. We are called to obey no unknown prophet but to accept the power and guidance of thy Son. The risen Christ strides on ahead of us, beckoning us to new ways of life and thought but offering us also new resources to accomplish his will. As long ago he said to his disciples, "None of you asketh me, Whither goest thou?" so he rebukes our unwillingness to ask where his living spirit beckons us. Open our eyes to those new adventures of friendship and forgiveness, those new paths of reconciliation, those new experiments of fearless trust to which he is summoning us in these new days.

Lord, we hear thee calling us to follow thee in breaking down barriers of race and class.

Lord, we hear thee calling us to follow thee in freeing the prisoners of agelong servitude, in creating sonship out of slavery, partnership out of paternalism.

Lord, we hear thee calling us to follow thee in finding unity with our Christian brothers across the world.

Lord, we hear thee calling us to create opportunities out of problems, to co-operate with thee in bringing new things to birth out of the old, and to follow where thy restless spirit is seeking to lead men in our time. Help us to respond to thy call.

And this we ask for Jesus Christ's sake.

Amen.

A Prayer for Freedom from Fear

Jesus said: Be of good cheer; it is I; be not afraid.

O God, whose Son Jesus Christ delivered men from fear in the days of his flesh and whose risen presence has led multitudes out of the darkness of superstition and error into thy marvelous light, help us to hear his strong voice summoning us from fear into trust.

Strengthen us when we fall into fear of public opinion, when we let the pressures of daily life harass and frighten us.

Uphold us when we become fearful of ourselves, unable to control our thoughts or to check our anxieties, and when we become victims of our undisciplined past.

Encourage us when we give way to fear of failure, when we brood over the haste of time and bewail the fact that we have done so little, when we meet every new task with foreboding, when we hesitate to attempt what we have come to feel is beyond our strength.

Hearten us when we entertain the fear of death, when the unknown seems to have no hope in it and our sins rise up to mock our confidence.

Rebuke us when we carry our fears into our prayers, when we refuse to accept thy forgiveness, and when we pay more heed to our own feelings than to the witness of Jesus Christ and his cross.

Forgive us for the fear in which we enwrap our loved ones, communicating to them our own distrust and robbing them of confidence in thy power.

Pardon us for the fears we bring into our church life, fears that tempt us to employ the strategies and tactics of the world, to use doubtful means for winning and holding men.

Have mercy upon us when we are afraid to launch out into the deep and paddle around the shallows of life, when we seek to preserve rather than to extend, to gather rather than to distribute, to secure our future rather than to step forth into thine.

And teach us to heed again the words of our trust-worthy Lord; to hear his "Fear not, little flock; for it is your Father's good pleasure to give you the king-dom." In the joy and power of that Kingdom equip us to face the uncertainties and alarms of life, knowing that nothing can take us out of the Father's hands.

And this we ask for Jesus Christ's sake.

AMEN.

A Prayer for Christian Discrimination

Jesus said: *Beware of false prophets.*

Almighty God, we pray for power to sift the wheat from the chaff amid the complexities of our daily life. Thou knowest that we are beset behind and before with words and promises, that we are offered panacea and solutions without number. Sometimes we are bewildered by the very variety of them; sometimes we are tempted to confuse the big with the small, to mistake propaganda for truth, and pretentiousness for profundity.

Enable us by thy searching spirit to detect the false from the true, and, above all, to choose what is genuine, for it is our greed and laziness that often lead us astray. We become attracted by what promises quick results and effortless response. Forgive us this sin.

Teach us to trust no hands that escape the print of the nails, to heed no voice that lacks the accent of Galilee.

And ground us in the love of Christ that we might become true prophets to our time, interpreting aright the signs of the times and guiding our fellow men into ways of fellowship and peace.

Teach us to exercise the prophetic ministry in our daily vocation, to expose what is flimsy by the solid work of our hands, to rebuke what is aimless by the strength of our purpose, to exalt what is honest and of good report by our delight in simple, enduring things.

Cleanse thy church of misguided and misguiding witnesses, create in us all the power to speak the interpretive word and to do the interpreting deed.

Grant us power, as communities and individuals, to cleanse our culture of attractive lies, to exalt the standards of youth, and to raise up a generation of scholars and teachers, of writers and entertainers whose aim it will be to "approve the things that are excellent."

Grant that in all things we may be guided and inspired by the life that was light, the life in whose acts and deeds we see most clearly the purpose of God for the life of the world.

And this we ask for Jesus' sake.

AMEN.

A Prayer for Abundant Life

Jesus said: *I am come that they might have life, and that they might have it more abundantly.*

Almighty and generous God, whose will for us is that we should be fully alive, alive to the splendor of the world, alive to the riches of personal relationships, alive to the adventure of being fully human, we turn to thee in this act of worship to confront anew thy promise of life in Jesus Christ.

We confess with shame that we have lived in poverty in the midst of plenty, preferring the austerity of the far country to the fullness of the Father's house.

Forgive us our reluctance to take thee at thy word.

We confess with sorrow that we have shut life out through fear and timidity. We have been afraid of vitality and have sought the safety of ordinariness. We have been happier with acquaintances than friends, with repetition than with new victories, with increase of reputation than with renewal of character. Forgive us our failure to accept life through growth and struggle.

We confess, above all, that our sins have made us incapable of welcoming abundant life. Selfishness has turned the open hand into the clenched fist. Lustful thoughts have blinded us to the grace of life. Envy and pride have shut us out of genuine friendship. Forgive us for clinging to these impoverishing sins, and encourage us anew to desire the life that is life indeed.

Send us forth into the world to encourage others to live abundantly. Forgive us when we become afraid for our children instead of teaching them to meet life with gestures of acceptance and trust. Rebuke us when we become more anxious to help men to live safely than to live boldly.

Make us shapers of a city, a community, a country wherein the life of the inhabitants is the paramount concern of civic leaders, editors, industrialists, artists, and statesmen. May all our social and political efforts tend to the creation of a land where men may freely love one another and find life in that love.

As members of thy Son's Church grant that his offer of life may be heard through our preaching, our worship, our fellowship, and save us from exalting the institution or the tradition over the needs and claims of the individual.

Help us to remember, today and always, those who languish in weakness of body, those whose physical vitalities are sapped through illness, those whose mental powers are dissipated through worry, those whose spiritual resources are at a low ebb through sin. Grant that we might be honored by the opportunity to help them in thy name.

These things we ask through Jesus Christ our Lord.

AMEN.

A Prayer for Repentance

Jesus said: *I am not come to call the righteous, but sinners to repentance.*

Almighty and forgiving God, we turn to thee in this act of worship, realizing afresh that we have no claim upon thee until we are real with ourselves.

If we have entered thy house congratulating our-

selves on our righteousness, secure in our own goodness, reveal to us the poverty of our accomplishments
and the infinite demands of thy love. In the presence
of thy Son Jesus Christ may we become aware of
the offense of our self-righteousness, our isolation from
our fellows, our failure to love our enemies, to forgive
our tormenters, and to esteem our fellow men more
than ourselves. Reveal to us the ambiguity of our
motives, the selfishness that has crept into our finest
actions, the fear that has dictated much of our
generosity and tolerance. Help us to measure our
giving by the self-giving of Christ and our sacrifice
by the agony of his cross.

Then, in thy mercy, call us to repentance. Help us
to turn again to thee, whose love alone can create
love in us. Help us to turn from our efforts at self-im-
provement to thee, whose righteousness is a consuming
and renewing fire. Help us to enter into the fellowship
with thee, whose kingdom of love, joy, and peace can
empower and enrich our little lives.

And being forgiven and restored, create in us the
passion to forgive and restore; make us capable of
sharing love with others, of fanning into life the
flame of repentance wherever we find it. Help us to
treat sinful men with the compassion and understanding of our Master and Lord, whose purity and goodness never created a barrier between him and his
fellow men.

We pray for thy Church, that she may be a fellowship of the forgiven and the forgiving, a redemptive society acting in a world where forgiveness is hard to come by. May all who enter this house realize with humble joy that they have come home, home to a Father and to sons who share the Father's passion for reconciliation.

Because we are set down in a world where men live by asserting thir superiority, by confessing other people's sins rather than their own, help us to bring a new spirit into our secular affairs. Teach us to acknowledge our guilt as members of parties, as citizens, as patriots, as husbands and wives, as children; grant that we may recover our unity in need and turn to thee who can create the unity of forgiveness.

This we ask for Jesus Christ's sake.

AMEN.

A Prayer for Fulfillment in Christ

Jesus said: *I am not come to destroy, but to fulfil.*

Almighty God, who art ever seeking the health and holiness of thy children, we, thy sons and daughters, are gratefully conscious of thy struggle with us. We have felt the pressure of thy spirit upon our partial lives, summoning us to fulfill our destinies and to be wholly thy children. Again and again thou hast unsettled our contentment, thou hast rebuked our readiness to remain unchallenged and unfulfilled. Because of thee our hearts are restless and our finest human achievements do not satisfy.

We believe thou art calling us to exercise our human powers to the full. Yet time and again we live at half-pressure because our aims are muddled and our loyalties are confused. Summon us anew to thy service that all our powers may flow in unison and strength, that our powers as craftsmen, workers, thinkers, planners, traders, and parents may flower into joy, and that our daily work may recreate and renew us.

We believe that thou art calling us to fulfill the potentialities of the flesh, to make our bodies a perfect vehicle for the spirit. Sometimes we are so frightened of the flesh that we seek to destroy it or to ignore it or to enchain it. Summon us anew to redeem it and, through the word made flesh, to create a living unity of body and spirit.

We believe thou art calling us to fulfill our humanity in the God-manhood of Jesus Christ, to be created anew in him. Help us to enter into the victory of his cross and resurrection that we might learn to live a dying and a rising life each day.

We believe thou art seeking the fulfillment of our

human institutions, seeking to turn our statutes into songs, our laws into grace, our legalism into love, our collectivities into communities, and our constraints into communion. Teach us so to lay hold on Christ that we might have power to bring to fruition the potentialities of every human being we meet and every human institution we belong to.

And save us, O God, from the impatience that would destroy, from the religious zeal that would spurn, the efforts of un-Christed men. Give us thine own unwearied passion to bring forth and to perfect what is good in men.

Give us deep sympathy with all who are depressed by unfulfilled hopes, all who despair of themselves, all who are tempted to give up the struggle for better things; may we live in their midst as followers of him who came, "not to destroy, but to fulfill."

We ask it for his name's sake.

AMEN.

A Prayer for Salvation

Jesus said: *The Son of Man is come to seek and to save that which was lost.*

O God, forgive us if these words mean little to us, if we are so much at home in the world that we do not recognize ourselves as lost.

We are not daring sinners or rebel souls; yet sometimes these words have a strange power to disturb us. Perhaps, after all, we are lost in our very safety, lost in our comfort, lost in our detachment, lost in our pride in not being lost.

If we have arrived at a state where the Son of man cannot reach us, if his humanity no longer quickens and excites us, are we not lost?

If his cross no longer moves us nor casts its healing shadow over our lives, are we not lost?

If we can hide even from thee, O disturbing God, within our securities of home, success, and conformity, are we not lost?

Help us, then, to examine anew our availability to thee.

Forgive us if we shelter from thee behind our smooth adjustment to the world.

Forgive us if we are lost to thee behind our religious orthodoxies and our ecclesiastical commitments.

Forgive us if we are insulated from thee within the walls of our satisfying, domestic life.

Forgive us if we are lost to thee within our conventionally respectable lives.

Forgive us if we are no longer willing to be sought and found by thy searching love.

Spare us, O Lord, from discovering our lostness through tragedy and frustration; send forth thy spirit now and rescue us from our detachment. Recall us to fellowship with thee that through thee we might discover the joy of belonging to each other. Suffer us not to drift into isolation like sheep, nor slip out of thy hand like the coin, nor cut ourselves off from the family like the son.

And help us, in turn, to care for the lost, to win men from selfish detachment for the joy of fellowship, to arouse in others the desire to belong to the larger family of mankind, and to relate their small concerns to the kingdom of thy Son.

Create in thy Church a share of thy seeking and saving love that we may look beyond our own walls and witness beyond our own small circle, becoming indeed a missionary church.

Help us to detect all that is lost and aimless in our civic and community life, all that, well begun, has lost its purpose and drive, and give us the humility to work within the body politic to recover its ideals, to strengthen its purpose, and so to claim its life for thee.

We ask it for the sake of Jesus Christ.

AMEN.

A Prayer for Cleansing

Jesus said: *I am come to send fire on the earth.*

Almighty God, whose love is a consuming fire, we pray for courage to thank thee for thy heat as well as for thy warmth, for thy rigor as well as for thy gentleness.

In our folly we have often asked for comfort when we needed rebuke; we have prayed for approval when we needed the scorching fire of thy scorn; we have forgotten that thou art of purer eyes than to behold iniquity.

But in our better moments we know that our only hope lies in thy continued hostility to our sins. And so we pray, albeit timorously, that thou wilt bring to nothing everything that is shoddy and mean and evasive in our lives. Teach us to behold thy frown as well as thy smile.

Cleanse us by the fire of thy love from all self-love, burn up the dross in our hearts, the lingering lust, and the smoldering selfishness.

And create in us the capacity for indignation as well as for sympathy. Help us to pray prayers of wrath, to burn with righteous anger against all that exploits youth, that takes advantage of credulity, that capitalizes on the weakness of the aged. Save us from the fear of appearing intolerant and from the desire to stand well in all men's eyes. Teach us that there is approval that is not worth having, and that there are enemies a good man ought to have. But grant, O God, that our indignation may be righteous, and that our opposition to wrong may be untinged with vindictiveness and fear.

Teach us not to be surprised if, like Christ's, our love divides as well as unites and if the Cross becomes a crossroads where men meet and part. Then, Lord, in thy mercy, increase thy hold upon us lest we waver. Teach us to care for thy approval above that of our fellows.

Hear us as we pray for our fellow Christians who are tempted to compromise with Caesar in order that the Church might have peace, for the Church in our own land when she is tempted to seek approval rather than to exercise judgment, and for individual Christians when they are tempted to lower their standards. But above all hear us as we pray for ourselves that we might be constrained by the love of Christ and not our human anger.

This we ask in his name and for his sake.

AMEN.

SECTION V

Litanies

A Litany of Thanksgiving—I

Minister: It is a good thing to give thanks unto the Lord, to show forth his lovingkindness in the morning and his faithfulness every night.

Praise him for this world, our home, and for every sign of his presence within it, for all that ministers to our bodies and delights the senses and uplifts the heart.

People: **We praise thee, O God our Creator, and affirm our joy in being thy children. Teach us to use thy gifts with reverence, to prosper without hardening of heart, and to honor thee with eye and hand and heart.**

Minister: Praise God for his other children, companions with us in the privileges and tasks of life. Praise him for human co-operation, for shared work and play, for sympathy and sensitiveness, for the tenderness of love and the enrichment of marriage and parenthood.

People: **We praise thee, O God our Father, and affirm our joy in human brotherhood. Teach us to honor all men, to seek the good** of our fellows, and to grow in understanding and appreciation and compassion.

Minister: Praise God for light shining in darkness, for joy in creative strife, for growth in struggle, for meaning wrestled for in mystery, and for challenge and opportunity at the heart of every difficulty.

People: **We praise thee, O God our Companion, and affirm our joy in being trusted with freedom and initiative. Teach us to be creative and bold, to seek the inner meaning of every problem, and to fear nothing but dishonoring thy trust.**

Minister: Praise God for the Sonship of Jesus Christ, for his conquest of our servile hearts, encouraging us to live as sons of the Father. Praise him for redemption and forgiveness and the new start in life and for rescuing us from aimless living and inward defeat and outward confusion.

People: **We praise thee, O God our Saviour, and affirm our joy in being created anew in Jesus Christ. Teach us to accept Christ's offer of pardon and peace and to live henceforth in the power of his cross.**

Minister: Praise God for the reality of his kingdom in the midst of time and for the Church which is the bearer of his kingdom. Praise him for communities of the faith throughout the world and for the priesthood of all believers ministering to the hurt and ignorance and loneliness of his children.

People: We praise thee, O God our Redeemer, and affirm our joy in our membership of thy Son's Church. Teach us to hear the word and do it, to break and share the bread of life, and to extend the fellowship we find here into the common ways of life.

All: Praise be unto thee, O Lord our God, from this time forth and for evermore. Amen.

A Litany of Thanksgiving—II

All: We praise thee, O God; we acknowledge thee to be the Lord. All the earth doth worship thee, the Father everlasting.

Minister: For creating us in thine own image, for entrusting us with reason, imagination, free-

154

dom, and creativity and so making us capable of fellowship with thee,

People: **We praise thee, O God; we acknowledge thee to be the Lord.**

Minister: For setting the solitary in families, for the ecstacy of love, the strength of friendship, and for the enlargement of life that comes through partnership in work and leisure,

People: **We praise thee, O God; we acknowledge thee to be the Lord.**

Minister: For the gift of teachers, for the institutions of learning and craftsmanship, for libraries, art galleries, theaters, and concert halls, and for the excitement of education, the surprise of new thoughts, and the discovery of vocations,

People: **We praise thee, O God; we acknowledge thee to be the Lord.**

Minister: For the wide horizons of travel, the meeting with other minds, and the gradual conquest of prejudice, for opportunity of leisure, and for pressure of work that has called forth strength we never knew we had,

People: **We praise thee, O God; we acknowledge thee to be the Lord.**

Minister: For Jesus Christ, present in the midst of his

Church, training and encouraging us to live together, for the fellowship that nurtures us in Christian graces and offers us opportunities of service,

People: **We praise thee, O God; we acknowledge thee to be the Lord.**

Minister: For all who, in the name of Christ, pioneer in the ways of reconciliation and blaze trails of adventurous living, for all who do the dirty work of the world with a sense of mission, and for the sake of Christ,

People: **We praise thee, O God; we acknowledge thee to be the Lord.**

Minister: For all who spur us on to hope in Christ and to live upon his bounty, for all who uphold us when we fall and bear with us when we fail, and for the grace of the Lord Jesus Christ opening to us the love of God in the fellowship of the Holy Spirit,

All: **We praise thee, O God; we acknowledge thee to be the Lord. All the earth doth worship thee, the Father everlasting. AMEN.**

A Litany of Thanksgiving—III

Minister: We call to remembrance the mercy of the Lord. As far as the East is from the West, so far hath he removed our transgressions from us.

Let us praise him for the wonder of forgiveness. Though we have offended against his holy laws, he has not destroyed us; though we have slighted his goodness, he has not forsaken us.

People: **We praise thee, O God, for thy patience with us, the children of men. We thank thee that thou art more anxious to win us for love than to punish us for sin and to bring us home to thyself than to guard thy dignity.**

Minister: Let us praise God for searching us out in the far country, for all the frustrating experiences of life that have brought us to our senses, and for the failure of sin to satisfy us.

People: **We praise thee, O God, for our rescue from a life of humiliation, defeat, and shame and for the instruments thou hast used to call us home—self-disgust, spiritual hunger, nostalgia for the good past, the prayers of** the faithful, and the ever-present activity of thy Holy Spirit.

Minister: Let us praise God for enabling us to use the mistakes and failures of the past to make us humbly dependent upon him for each day's victory, to cast ourselves upon his grace, and to look to him for strength.

People: **We praise thee, O God, and learn anew the humility of the prayer, "Give us this day our daily bread." Teach us to see in this a new day with new opportunities for trusting thee and walking in thy love and sharing thy compassion.**

Minister: Let us praise God for Jesus Christ, in whom our forgiveness is assured through the wonder of his cross and resurrection, and without whom we would not dare to believe in the divine forgiveness.

People: **We praise thee, O God, for our confidence in thy love, awakened in us by the life and death and resurrection of Jesus Christ, for the good news that would be too good to be true if his cross did not placard it before our eyes and his voice did not invite us to take the step of faith.**

Minister: Let us praise God for the power of forgiveness to create new life, and especially for

the power granted to us to exercise forgiveness in Christ's name, and so to become the
instruments of reconciliation.

People: **We praise thee, O God, for releasing us
from guilt and remorse and shame and for
granting us the power to forgive others.
Teach us day by day to create hope among
the hopeless, to be sparing in condemnation
and generous with sympathy, and to share
with others the power of pardon that has
come to us in Jesus Christ. AMEN.**

A Litany of Praise and Penitence

Minister: O God, we praise thee that thy Son Jesus
Christ has opened the Kingdom of heaven
to all believers, that by his life and death
and resurrection he has created a new and
living way into fullness of life.

People: **Forgive us if we have preferred the old
to the new, half life to full life, and our
own achievements to his proffered gift.**

Minister: We praise thee that he lived in such unity with thee that his words are thy word to us, his compassion manifests thy love, and that in him we find the meaning of our own lives.

People: **Forgive us if we have ignored his teaching, slighted his love, and sought the meaning of life apart from him.**

Minister: We praise thee that on the Cross thy Son wrestled with the dark forces of this world and triumphed over them that we might share his victory and strength.

People: **Forgive us if we have run away from the difficult decisions of life, evading the Cross and missing the crown.**

Minister: We thank thee for his resurrection and the power of his endless life and for his risen presence summoning us to new commitment and surrender.

People: **Forgive us if we have sought him in the tomb of the past, if we have lived upon historical memory and nostalgia rather than on present experience and hope.**

Minister: We praise thee for the Church, his body, re-formed and renewed by his life within, breaking down barriers and committed to the ministry of reconciliation.

People: **Forgive us if we have used the Church to perpetuate privilege and to safeguard a cherished way of life or if we have sought to limit its influence.**

Minister: We praise thee for thy presence in the world beyond the Church, in the longing for national righteousness, for civic health, for true education, for better homes, for honorable industry, and for richer partnership among races, peoples, and classes.

People: **Forgive us if we have failed to see the signs of thy appearing in the common life or refused to take our part in co-operating with thy spirit.**

Minister: We praise thee, O God, and pray for grace to praise thee better.

All: **Amen.**

A Litany of Praise and Confession

Minister: Almighty God, by whose creative spirit we are sustained, by whose holy spirit we are cleansed every day, and by whose peaceful spirit our restlessness is calmed,

People: **We give thee thanks for the power of thy spirit in our midst.**

Minister: We recall the inspiration of thy spirit mediated to us through seers and prophets, through scriptures and preaching, through sacraments and fellowship, in the liveliness of conversation, in the inner solitude of secret struggle, and above all in our encounter with thy Son Jesus Christ.

People: **We give thee thanks for his presence in our midst.**

Minister: Because his life has quickened our life, because his perfect holiness has rebuked the shame and shabbiness of our lives and his grace abounded where most our sin abounded,

People: **We give thee thanks for his renewing and redeeming power.**

Minister: And since every remembrance of thy mercy recalls our ingratitude, our hearts cry out for forgiveness. Forgive the stubborn self-will that has resisted the offer of thy help, the foolish independence that sought to live in isolation from thee, and the pride that refused to say, "Thy will be done."

People: **Have mercy upon us, O God; have mercy upon us, and renew a right spirit within us.**

Minister: Forgive us the thoughts that strayed to forbidden things; forgive us the words that escaped in anger and malice; forgive us the deeds that expressed our fear and frustration more than our confidence in thee.

People: **Have mercy upon us, O God; have mercy upon us, and restore unto us the joy of thy salvation.**

Minister: For every occasion when we have sold our birthright and betrayed our manhood, succumbed to the luxury of self-pity, deserted our post of duty, and evaded our responsibility,

People: **We pray thy forgiveness, O God, and seek newness of life.**

Minister: Let us turn again with confidence to him who loved us, and loosed us from our sins and hath made us kings and priests unto God and his Father.

All: **Lord hear our prayer, and let our cry come unto thee. Amen.**

A Litany of Confession

Minister: Almighty God, whose Son Jesus Christ has revealed the nature of our sin by his perfect righteousness, we gather today under the judgment of his words. We are lost sheep, lost coins, lost sons; we are salt without savor, light hidden under a bushel, leaven out of touch with the lump; we are forgiven debtors who are reluctant to show forgiveness, children who will not play unless we can call the tune. We have built our house upon the sand; we have answered yes and acted no; we have prayed within ourselves in isolation and pride.

People: **Hear us, O Lord, and help us to bear thy word.**

Minister: Heavenly Father, who hast given us the Word made flesh, we stand today under the judgment of his life. We have lived without a baptism into all sorts and conditions of men; we have run away from the hour of testing in the wilderness; we have avoided the cries of hungry men and shirked the responsibility of teaching and healing. We have evaded the necessity of sacrifice; we have sought to bypass the Cross, and, above all, we have failed to live in newness of life with the risen Christ.

People: **Have mercy upon us, O Lord, and enable us to lay hold of the life that is life indeed.**

Minister: O God, who hast called us into the Church of thy Son, we recall with shame that we have forsaken the assembling of ourselves together in love, that we have been guilty of divisions, that we have heard the preaching of the word without obedience, that we have broken bread without discerning the Lord's body and have weakened the fellowship through hardness of heart, through failure of imagination, and through pride and vain glory.

People: **Restore unto us the joy of thy salvation and uphold us with thy free spirit.**

Minister: God so loved the world that whosoever believeth in him should not perish but have everlasting life. Let us hear and receive this word of invitation.

All: **Accept us, O Lord, and deliver us from all our sins, through thy Son Jesus Christ. Amen.**

A Litany of Deliverance

Minister: Almighty God, who didst deliver thine ancient people from slavery and in the fullness of time didst send thy Son Jesus Christ to deliver the people from their sins, hear us as we pray for deliverance from our bondage and lead us forth into the glorious liberty of the children of God.

People: **Hear our prayer, O Lord, and let our cry come unto thee.**

Minister: Deliver us from satisfaction with slavery, from willing bondage to the flesh, from contentment with mediocrity, and from our reluctance to enter the kingdom of God.

People: **Hear our prayer, O Lord, and lead us forth into the land of promise.**

Minister: Deliver us from fragmentary living, from divided aims and rival loyalties, and from failure to seek and achieve wholeness in thought, word, and deed.

People: **Teach us to pray, "Seek ye first the Kingdom of God and all else shall be added unto you."**

Minister: Deliver us from counterfeit humility, from the modesty that calls attention to itself, from the arrogance which creates the world in our own image, and will not bow to the authority of truth as it meets us in Jesus Christ.

People: **Hear our prayer, O Lord, and save us from ourselves.**

Minister: Deliver us from religious selfishness, from the piety that is centered upon safety rather than service, from seeking peace of mind instead of reconciliation with thee and with all men.

People: **Teach us to say, "He that loseth his life for my sake shall find it.**

Minister: Deliver us from being sorry for ourselves and not for our sins, for esteeming reputation above character and the show of righteousness above the reality of it.

People: **O God, create in us a clean heart, and renew a right spirit within us.**

Minister: Deliver us, above all, from substituting religion for Christ, from taking refuge in systems and ceremonies that bring us comfort and security rather than encountering his disturbing presence.

All: **Thou, O Christ, art all we want,**
More than all in thee we find. Amen.

A Litany of Intercession—I

Minister: Heavenly Father, who hast bound us in the bundle of life with other people and taught us to pray for all sorts and conditions of men, we pray for sympathy and understanding, for imaginative insight into peoples' needs, and for the power of brotherhood that comes from abiding in thy fatherly love.

People: **Holy Father, in thy mercy hear our prayer and enlarge our sympathy.**

Minister: In the name of Jesus Christ we pray for those who are smitten with sickness, with weariness of body and mind, for those who are bearing burdens thrust upon them by circumstances and are ready to faint, and for those who are forced to show cheerfulness in the face of tragedy.

People: **Help us to pray, "Bear ye one another's burdens, and so fulfill the law of Christ."**

Minister: We pray for those who are carrying burdens of their own making, for those who are shut up in the hollow world of self-pity or crippled by remorse they cannot share with thee, and for all who suffer from depression and look out upon the world with jaundiced eyes.

People: **O Lord, hear our prayer, and let our cry come unto thee.**

Minister: We pray for all who are bitter in spirit, inflicting pain on others because they are hurt and bewildered, for those who are seeking recognition by outrageous conduct and sarcastic speech, for all who seek revenge on society by refusing to co-operate.

People: **O Lord, hear our prayer and let our cry come unto thee.**

Minister: Let us pray for words to restore self-respect and to awaken hope, for sensitiveness to know the time to speak and the time to be silent, for courage to be frank and the ability to speak the truth in love.

People: **O Lord, open thou our lips, and our mouths shall show forth thy praise.**

Minister: Let us pray for freedom from self and such commitment to Christ and his Kingdom as will liberate us to be perpetual intercessors, living for and with other people in the name of the Lord Jesus Christ.

People: **O Lord, direct our lives and use them to convict, to rebuke, and to heal.**

All: **Amen.**

A Litany of Intercession—II

Minister: O God, who hast set the solitary in families and given us happiness in one another, we thank thee that the deepest joys are those we share with others. We give thee thanks for the enrichment and support of love and marriage and parenthood, for the blessings of friendship, and for the claims of duty and responsibility that quicken our humanity.

People: **Thanks be unto thee, O God.**

Minister: We lift up our hearts in intercession for the lonely, the bereaved, for those who are torn away from those they love, and especially for those who have created loneliness for themselves through pride and fear.

People: **O Lord, strengthen us to help and restore the needy.**

Minister: We pray for the oversensitive, for men and women born with one skin too few, for those who feel the irritations of life as though they were calamities, and for those who are driven in upon themselves.

People: **O God, help us to share with them the vision of the Kingdom of God.**

Minister: We pray for men and women unhappily yoked together, making the best of a bad job, for those forced by circumstances to remain single, and for all who feel themselves to be misfits and unwanted, and for all who carry despair into every situation and so make it worse.

People: **O God, help us to restore courage and human dignity by our own purposeful living.**

Minister: We pray for all who labor in uncongenial places, for those who cannot find a vocation in their work, and for those who feel sullied by the ideas and conversation of their workmates yet have no positive word of witness to speak.

People: **O God, help us to convince them that there is grace to help in every time of need.**

Minister: And finally let us pray for those who are strong and have not learned to share their strength, for those who are impatient with the problems of others, and for those who have all the answers and will not listen to the questions.

People: **Give us, we beseech thee, the listening ear, the heart at leisure from itself to soothe and sympathize, for Jesus Christ's sake.**

All: **Amen.**

A Litany of Intercession—III

Minister: Almighty God, whose Fatherhood binds us to all men, we join in prayer for all who are knit to us by ties of blood, for our loved ones at home and abroad, for those who dwell under our roof and sometimes seem very far away, and for those who live under distant skies yet are never far from our thoughts.

People: **Holy Father, in thy mercy hear our prayer.**

Minister: We pray for all who are joined to us in friendship, whom we long to help in their struggle for self-mastery, for better health, and for a more satisfying life. We pray for those who cannot see a meaning in the pain they bear, in the loneliness they endure, or in the burdens they carry.

People: **Holy Father, in thy mercy hear our prayer.**

Minister: We pray for the enemies we have created through our pride, our clumsiness, or our unconscious jealousy, for the misunderstanding that has alienated us from colleagues, workmates, or partners.

People: **Holy Father, in thy mercy hear our prayer.**

Minister: For all who labor to create a cleaner society,

a more united nation, a better world and
who, by pen or brush or voice or skillful
fingers, enrich the culture and ease the
burden of the world,

People: **Holy Father, in thy mercy hear our prayer.**

Minister: For those who scorn delights and live labo-
rious days to give themselves to the better-
ment of their fellows and for those who
assist the heroes and pioneers behind the
scenes,

People: **Holy Father, in thy mercy hear our prayer.**

Minister: For those who teach the young to choose
wisely, for all who renew the desire for
learning in the mature, and for those who
impart new skills to the old,

People: **Holy Father, in thy mercy hear our prayer.**

Minister For all who, in Christ's name, transcend the
barriers of age and learning, race and color,
temperament and training to draw all into
the fellowship of reconciliation,

People: **Holy Father, in thy mercy hear our prayer.**

All: **Amen.**

A Litany of Intercession—IV

Minister: O God, whose Son Jesus Christ has made us members one of another, we take our place in the human family by offering our prayers for our brothers and sisters in Christ. We pray for those who have given up praying for themselves, because experience has made them cynical or wary of asking, for those who dislike what they have become but will not turn to thee for forgiveness, and for those who have made an uneasy peace with conscience.

People: **Lord, hear our prayer, and strengthen us to be a strength to others.**

Minister: We pray for those who are weakened by selfishness and poisoned by resentment, for those who see every man's hand against them, and for those who are intent on spoiling the peace of others.

People: **Lord, hear our prayer, and make us the instruments of thy peace.**

Minister: We pray for those who exploit the weak, for those who manipulate the curiosity and vitality of youth for sordid gain, and for those who prey upon the fear of the anxious and the credulity of the ignorant.

People: **Lord, hear our prayer, and make us instruments of thy wrath.**

Minister: We pray for the disgruntled, the weak-minded, the one talent men who bury their gift, the sick who have taken refuge in invalidism, and the bereaved who have lost the power of making new friends.

People: **Lord, hear our prayer, and make us the instruments of thy renewal.**

Minister: We pray for all who strive to win men back to health of body and mind, for those who refuse to be discouraged by failure, for those who live in the midst of negative thoughts and pessimism and hopelessness yet remain undaunted.

People: **Lord, hear our prayer, and enable us to join their ranks.**

Minister: Finally, we pray for ourselves, that in the name and power of Christ we may bring healing to the sick, hope to the defeated, and confidence to the disheartened.

All: **Lord, hear our prayer and make us the children of thy love, through Jesus Christ our Lord. Amen.**

A Litany of Petition

Minister: O God, we bring our needs and desires into thy presence, but we are conscious that our greatest need is to be awakened to needs of which we are not conscious. We pray for finer ambitions, for deeper longings, for stronger commitment to thy purpose, and for greater awareness of our radical dependence upon thee.

People: **Out of the depths we cry unto thee, O Lord, Lord, hear our prayer.**

Minister: If the urgencies of the flesh have swamped the needs of the spirit, if self-care has made us careless of the claims of others, or if the day's demands have made us forget the demands of the eternal.

People: **Out of the depths we cry unto thee, O Lord, Lord, hear our prayer.**

Minister: If we seek for private satisfactions, forgetting the needs of society, if we pray for *our* church, forgetting the Church universal, if we are dedicated to class, race, or nation, forgetting the claims of mankind,

People: **Out of the depths we cry unto thee, O Lord, Lord, hear our prayer.**

Minister: If we love those who love us, if we serve those who appreciate our service, if we forgive those who are dear to us, forgetting that love knows no limits,

People: **Out of the depths we cry unto thee, O Lord, Lord, hear our prayer.**

Minister: If we have tried to make do with minimum faith, minimum duties, minimum service, forgetting the infinite claims of thy holy love upon us,

People: **Out of the depths we cry unto thee, O Lord, Lord, hear our prayer.**

Minister: If we have confused conformity with obedience, if we have been satisfied with nominal churchmanship, if we have not hungered and thirsted after righteousness,

People: **Out of the depths we cry unto thee, O Lord, Lord, hear our prayer.**

Minister: If we have localized our discipleship, if we have restricted our Christian life to limited areas, if we have allowed Christ to be Lord only on the surface of life,

People: **Out of the depths we cry unto thee, O Lord, Lord, hear our prayer, and let our prayer come unto thee. Amen.**

A Litany of Dedication

Minister: Almighty God, we gather today to dedicate ourselves anew to the love that is ever seeking fuller entrance into our hearts.
We thank thee that we are called into the fellowship and service of Jesus Christ, and that he is able and willing to use us to proclaim the kingdom of his love.

People: **We dedicate our gifts of speech, conversation, and writing to the cause of peace, love, and reconciliation.**

Minister: We thank thee that we are called to use the work of our hands, the opportunities of professional and business life, the vocation of parenthood, sonship, and home-building to share with others the love of Christ.

People: **We dedicate our gifts of skill, integrity, and craftsmanship to the cause of friendship and fuller Christian living.**

Minister: We thank thee that we are called into the Church of Jesus Christ to extend his healing reign, to keep alive the conscience of the world, and to carry out his commission.

People: **We dedicate our gifts of leadership, teaching, stewardship, and friendship to the cause of true community and the awakening of life in others.**

Minister: We thank thee that we are called into conversation with men and women of other faiths, other denominations, other nationalities in the name and the spirit of the one Great Shepherd who wills that all should belong to him.

People: **We dedicate our denominational insights and treasures to the one Church and seek humbly to learn from all who profess faith in Christ.**

Minister: We thank thee that we are called to share with all men, irrespective of creed, class, or color, what we have gained from Christ, disdaining none, patronizing none, and misrepresenting none.

All: **We dedicate our gifts of persuasion, conviction, and experience to the human family, seeking the good of all and the triumph of the Kingdom of God. Amen.**

A Litany of Renewal and Hope

Minister: O God, whose Son Jesus Christ triumphed over sin and death, we meet this day in expectation of his renewing power among us. We have been in bondage to sin and fearful of death, but now we would repent of our lack of faith and ask to be grasped anew by his conquering life.

People: Lord, hear our prayer, and let our cry come unto thee.

Minister: Assure our hearts that there is no place, no event, no meeting upon which we enter alone, and that we may confidently expect the risen Christ to create new occasions out of the familiar stuff of daily life.

People: Lord, hear our prayer, and renew a right spirit within us.

Minister: Give us power to enliven and invigorate our tired world, to bring courage into our politics, freshness into our homes, friendship into our business, and adventure into our church life.

People: Create in us a clean heart, O God, and renew a right spirit within us.

Minister: As members of thy Son's Church grant us freedom to move into the unknown and the untried in his name, to see the opportunities of the new day, and to serve the present age with its emerging problems and new needs.

People: **Help us to pray, "Thy Kingdom come on earth."**

Minister: Help us to see that Kingdom already in our midst and to live in continual expectation of its fuller entrance into our hearts and homes so that we may do all things in hope and be undiscouraged by delay.

People: **Lord, hear our prayer, and let our cry come unto thee.**

Minister: Because eternity has entered and transfigured our temporal existence through the resurrection of Christ, help us to acknowledge death as the entrance to a larger and fuller life. In this faith help us to meet both life and death, giving thee all the glory and all the praise.

All: **For thine is the kingdom and the power and the glory, both now and forever. Amen.**

SECTION VI

Offertory Prayers

O God, the giver of every good and perfect gift, give us skill and imagination to use the gifts which we now place on thy holy table. May this money be used by dedicated hands to further thy Kingdom, to create fellowship, and to bring the healing power of the gospel into the lives of men.

Lord of all life, as we place this money before thee, teach us the responsible use of all our gifts. Save us from wasting our substance in foolish living, save us from squandering great gifts on trivial ends, and deliver us from making money a barrier rather than a bridge between man and man.

O God, bless, if thou canst, the ways in which we have earned this money, and accept our thanks for all honorable means of earning a living. Help us to seek work that is its own reward, in which we grow in inward grace and strength and in the doing of which we find fellowship with others.

Lord, as we offer these material gifts for the service of thy Kingdom, deliver us both from the contempt of money and the overvaluing of it. May we use it with reverence for the enrichment of life and not its impoverishment.

O Lord, behind this offering lies the busy world of our working life—the factory, the shop, the office, the foundry, and the mill. So we ask thy blessing upon the industrial and commercial life of our city. Save us from creating a world where wealth accumulates and men decay.

Lord God, this offering is for the service of thy house. Help us not to negate it by using our time, talents, possessions, and wealth as though they had no religious significance. May all our spending and saving, our giving and sharing, meet with thy approval.

O God, as we place this money upon the altar, we bring together the sacred and the secular, the material and the spiritual, work and worship. Help us to use all our gifts to unify life and not to split it apart, to create fellowship and not to disrupt it.

Save us, O God, from making these gifts a substitute for the gift of ourselves. Rather, may they be the outward tokens of an inward commitment, an act of total self-giving, for Jesus Christ's sake.

O God, who has taught us that it is more blessed to give than to receive, increase in us the power of giving, the joy of giving, and the wisdom of giving. Teach us to distinguish between giving and spending that enriches life and the giving and spending that impoverishes it.

With these gifts, for the work and witness of this church, we offer our prayers for the one Church of Jesus Christ throughout all the world.

O Lord, who hast taught us to pray "Thy kingdom come," we offer and present these gifts that they may be used to extend thy healing reign. Bless the varied ministries of the members of this church—teachers, doctors, nurses, administrators, and businessmen— that together they may serve as agents of thy coming.

Lord, teach us so to live and work that all our ways may be prosperous and fruitful. Help us so to use the talents thou hast given to us that we may be entrusted with greater responsibilities and empowered with greater ability. Save us from hoarding life, and enable us to honor thee in all that we do.

Lord God, we thank thee for the privilege of giving, without which our lives would be impoverished indeed. We pray for grace to give well, to help without patronizing, to assist without weakening, to share without diminishing the self-respect of others.

O Lord, who hast taught us that the love of money is the root of all evil, teach us to care for what money can buy—not security but opportunity, not withdrawal from the world but a fuller participation within it, not prestige but use. Help us to handle all the goods of life in the same spirit as thy Son, who, out of his poverty, made many rich.

Lord, with these gifts we offer our thanks to thee for the varied ministries of the Church that shelters us—for the power of the Word and the strength of the sacraments, for the beauty of flowers on the altar, for the inspiration of music, for the encouragement of the fellowship of kindred spirits, and for the challenge of living, working, and praying with unkindred spirits.

O Lord, who needest not our gifts, for the cattle on a thousand hills are thine, we thank thee that thou dost permit us to share thy purposes and dost honor us by enlisting our aid.

Almighty God, as we bring these gifts for the work of this congregation in this city, we remember our neighbors united with us under the same sign of the Cross. Strengthen our corporate witness that the civic, commercial, and cultural life of our city may be enriched and strengthened thereby.

Lord, as we pray for a blessing upon the work of this church, we pray also for thy blessing upon the preaching and testimony of thy servants—army, navy, and air force chaplains, chaplains to schools and colleges, rescue workers, social workers, and those who minister to the sick in body and mind.

Lord, we thank thee that material things like bread and wine may carry sacramental meanings. We pray that this money which we now offer thee may speak of spiritual concern and friendship and so point beyond itself to the Great Giver of every good and perfect gift.

Lord, as we bring these gifts for thy blessing, we pray a blessing also upon our daily life. Redeem our work from drudgery, our spending from folly, our saving from meanness, and give us grace to receive as graciously as we give.

Lord, with these gifts, we reaffirm our membership of this thy church. Help us to belong to it in spirit and in truth and in deep inwardness.

189

INDEX OF SCRIPTURE

INDEX

ACTS OF WORSHIP